GATEWAY

To A

NEW

WORLD

ALSO BY PAULINE EDWARD

Aquarius: The Age of Revelation, Choice and Transformation

The Healing of Humanity

The Movement of Being

Choosing the Miracle

Leaving the Desert: Embracing the Simplicity of A Course in Miracles

Making Peace with God: The Journey of a Course in Miracles Student

Astrological Crosses: Exploring the Cardinal, Fixed and Mutable Modes

Everyday Numerology: Yearly Planning Made Easy, new version of *The Power of Time: Understanding the Cycles of Your Life's Path*

Gateway
To A
New
World

Pauline Edward

Desert Lily Publications
Montreal, Canada

Copyright © 2024 Pauline Edward
Published by Desert Lily Publications, Montreal, Canada
All rights reserved. No part of this work may be reproduced or used in any form or by any means, electronic, digital or mechanical, including photocopying, recording or any retrieval system, without the prior written permission of the publisher.

Paperback ISBN 978-1-927694-13-8
Hardcover ISBN 978-1-927694-20-6

Cover design and layout: Pauline Edward
Poems by Michael J. Miller

Contents

Foreword vii
Preface ix
1. The First Step 1
2. Our Place in the Cosmos 21
3. The Demise of the God of Old 37
4. Reknowing God 53
5. Once Upon a Time 75
6. Finding Hope 97
7. Home Away from Home 117
8. Reunification 137
9. Standing at the Gateway 159
10. Sowing the Seeds 179
Bibliography 201
About the Author 202
Acknowledgments 203
Reviews 204

Foreword

I have only known Pauline for a short time, but I feel like we share a soul connection that transcends the limited amount of earth time we have been in contact. She found me by way of the book I have been reading on my podcast, *The Jeshua Channelings*, which is a mutual favorite of ours! This collection of channelings has provided some of the most profound inspirations and joy-filled moments, given my long journey from Christianity, which consumed the first 37 years of life, to Atheism for a few years, to this new, undefined, expansive space I am beginning to explore. Pauline and I were destined to meet, as two ex-religious people striving to embrace the expansive, infinite love that Jeshua describes, while releasing the stifling, limiting energies of the soul seeking to discover its true nature.

Pauline has been very gracious with her time and knowledge, as she spent a good 2 hours helping me understand a bit of my astrological chart over a video call. She provided me with great encouragement and the potential for a bright path ahead, should I choose to embrace it. She also informed me she was writing a new book, and asked if I wanted to read the manuscript. I was flattered and honored, and I had a very good feeling based on our conversation that it was going to be right up my alley!

When I read *Gateway to a New World*, it felt like a perfect companion to *The Jeshua Channelings*. One of the things I really love about this book, and that stirs me deeply, is Pauline's vulnerable, honest approach to her past. She shares the truth about her journey of setting aside the old, patriarchal, limiting language of the God of her upbringing, and connecting to new language and understanding of, as she puts it, Pure Life, or Creator Source. She has had many interesting "spiritual" experiences that add to the profundity of her journey.

Pauline's history with astrology and her devotion to learning as much about it as possible, really shines in this book. It helps us understand aspects of the new Aquarius energy that is on the planet at this time, as well as how we got here, from an energetic and planetary alignment perspective. Pauline is helping contextualize why things have been the way they are, and how differently things will be as we move forward. She toes the line gracefully, sharing relevant and helpful information about the astrological aspects, without beating you over the head with info, leaving you scratching your head, and feeling unsure about what you just read.

This book just fits so perfectly, and is so synchronous with many other sources/authors/channels I have been tapping into lately, that I can't help but feel a sense of awe to even be a part of it in any way. There is a movement of remembrance, of reconnection to our innate divinity that is starting to gain a lot of traction, and Pauline is one of the courageous, frontline people, sharing her vision of the New World. I for one am more than ready to join in this choir of hope and self-actualization, and this book is a great guide for this grand journey we are all on as humans, and furthermore as souls and spirits.

For me though, the grand culmination of this work is one of the most simple concepts that Pauline describes plainly and simply. We do not give the love to ourselves that we give to others, or that we want for others. She mentions in the book how shockingly low the percentage of people she encountered, when asked directly, had ever truly paused, reflected, and applied the love they try to give out to the world, to themselves! It's a stark statistic, because most of us associate self-love and forgiveness with an ego trip, or a warped perspective. Nothing could be further from the truth, and I am so happy that this was a central theme that Pauline honed in on perfectly, with this wonderfully encouraging and inspiring book. Now off to read her back catalog!

David O'Donnell
Creator of the podcast: *you are the One you seek*

Preface

We know that every time one of you meditates, every time one of you writes in your journal, every time one of you smiles at a stranger, humanity moves forward. There is a cumulative effect, a synergy of these events and these energies that occurs, especially when they are all happening simultaneously. (The 9D Arcturian Council, channelled by Daniel Scranton)

Those who are familiar with my previous books know how writing has been an integral part of my journey in this life, probably in other lifetimes too, therefore it's not something I am likely to abandon anytime soon. Ideas or flashes of insight usually come to me during the night, very early in the morning, or while I'm out walking rather than at convenient times, like when I'm actually at the computer. As I want to capture these snippets before they fade from memory—and they fade very quickly!—I keep a recorder next to my bed and always take it along when I go for walks. These little snippets of information and guidance are so important to me that the recordings are then dictated into the computer, backed up on a flash drive and a couple of external hard drives, and then printed and stored in a binder. I know, quirky process, perhaps even neurotic, but that's what works for me.

The reason for all of this quirkiness is that, at least for me, journalling seems to open the doorway to knowledge, wisdom, and guidance that I might not otherwise have access to given the noise and busyness of day-to-day life. As insights emerge from the quiet place within, the way forward is made clearer, greater understanding arises, answers to questions and solutions to problems—usually very simple, even obvious solutions—suddenly pop up, and more appropriate choices can then be made. So it is that I have come to appreciate this note-gathering process as an invaluable and cherished tool on this great journey of life.

While organizing material in preparation for the writing of this book, I pulled out my oldest journal, hand-written during what I referred to as the "dark night of the soul" period of my life. Never underestimate the value of good penmanship! Having long forgotten those journal entries, I was unexpectedly touched by the opening paragraph, dated January 2, 1975 (age 20).

> Once again I have the urge to write some of those very thoughts that go through my head. The more I read books, the more I want to write. This feeling for writing goes back at least six or seven years [age 13–14!]. I've always respected writers of all kinds, maybe because I could never write half the required number of pages in school assignments. I would get straight to the point in question, without any flowery descriptions.

A few weeks later, I made the following entry: "I have a burning desire to write a book!" As I read that young, naive soul's heartfelt words, I couldn't help but love the long-lost child in me. Clearly, I thought, young people should be encouraged to keep a journal so that one day they may look back and, instead of seeing defects and mistakes, they will feel love for the brave child who stepped into the world in this most challenging of times.

Throughout my life, many words have been captured—the large pile of notebooks, binders, discs and drives being a testament to that fact. As writing is clearly a significant part of my journey, I continue to put ink to paper and, of course, bits and bytes onto drives. However, it did take a few decades—okay, more like half a century—for me to accept that writing books, that is, sharing some of my insights and experiences with readers, is also an integral part of my function in this lifetime—at least for now—so, moving write along...

PREFACE

Besides my astrology and numerology books, *Astrological Crosses* and *The Power of Time*, and a brave attempt at writing a novel many, many years ago, this is the seventh book in which I share my seemingly insatiable quest to uncover the true meaning of life. Starting with *Making Peace with God*, the books leading up to this one describe a search that began with the traditional Roman Catholic doctrines of my youth, moving on through Eastern, metaphysical, philosophical, theosophical, occult, shamanic, esoteric, New Age and contemporary spiritual teachings. Perhaps I should say my quest for an actual experience of truth, because I have come to "understand" that intellectual understanding, no matter how comprehensive—although a valuable and helpful part of the process—is meaningless without the confirmation of that "inner knowing." And that true, inner knowing can only be acquired through personal, first-hand experience, a most valuable asset, as we shall see, in the newly emerging Era of Aquarius.

Clearly, not everyone is cut out for the writing life—book writing, that is. As I like to say, writing is rewriting and, to paraphrase Hemingway, the first draft is always shit. Writing a book is indeed a lot of work; way more work than simple journalling. After several decades of experience, I can say that it does get a bit easier with time and practice, but it is still a lot of work. Fortunately for me, writing suits my monk-like personality, which is not the case for everyone.

In spite of my inherently reclusive nature, I have agreed to continue to share some of my personal experiences in my writing. While being clearly urged by inner guidance to pursue this path, this also seems to be what my readers like best. Those familiar with my previous books know that, for the most part, my life has been rather simple and uneventful. However, over the past couple of years I have had a few unusual experiences, which are shared in this book. These were definitely not easy to describe in words, but I have done my best to convey them as clearly as possible for the reader. If my writings can be of help for a handful of souls, then I will have served my purpose, and for me, this is a purpose for which there is no greater honour.

That being said—or, written—the reader should keep in mind that writing does not make a person special. Also, because someone writes, it does not mean that they know what is right for you. Only you know that. In fact, everyone has a book inside of them since, as an expression of the unlimited fountain of Life, everyone has an original, valid, and meaningful story to tell. If, while reading something, the bells go off and the content seems to resonate with you or perhaps triggers a reaction, know that the words are simply confirming or mirroring back the wisdom or a challenge or a learning opportunity that you carry deep inside. Ultimately, each soul comes to realize that truth resides within; it has never been withheld nor can it ever be withheld. In fact, the truth simply waits for when we are ready to let it in.

There are many ways of sharing a soul's journey besides writing; in fact, there are as many ways as there are souls. Some will share their story through ordinary daily social interactions, and others through various forms of creative or artistic expression. Some may share their soul's passion through a job, career, business venture or profession that is dear to their heart. But more importantly, regardless of our function or position, we constantly share who and what we are through our everyday exchanges with others and by extension, with the world. It is each person's unique, individual soul expression that makes life rich, fascinating, expansive and colourful for all. Together we learn, grow, and contribute to the healing and transformation of all life on Earth.

As mentioned in my previous books, it is not necessary to have read my earlier works before reading this one. Feel free to jump right in if you have been called to it. On this rapidly changing journey of life, it makes sense to get on the train at the station nearest you. Only the destination is the same: the full conscious experience and expression of Being. Also, in the last couple of years, I have learned a few things that can help make the way clearer, even easier. In this complicated, challenging, and oftentimes confusing world, "easy" may be very much appreciated. As more souls are becoming aware, we have quite the journey ahead of us as we aim for a world of higher consciousness, love, compassion, inclusiveness, harmony, freedom, peace and equality for all. A key point on this journey is that we will attain our goal as we work *together*. So, get on the train and help us move forward.

What may seem a bit challenging at times is the fact that there are as many paths Home as there are paths that lead away from Home—Home being the full experience of who and what we truly are, the full experience of Being. So, in the matter of this emerging and expanding awareness, or any life experience for that matter, there is no one-size-fits-all formula. By the same token, if a particular path appeals to you, it does not make you any more advanced or successful or "awake" than one for whom that path holds no appeal. Whether or not it includes a spiritual, scientific, artistic, traditional, psychological, philosophical, religious, intellectual, metaphysical, cultural, or practical component, any path that leads to the full conscious awareness of Being is worthy of your attention, and in the end, that's all that matters.

While these writings express snippets of one person's journey, it does not mean that others must, or even should, pursue the same path. Thank goodness! And that's good news. Who wants to keep studying and researching and digging and questioning as I did throughout this life! It is time for a shift, and this can only occur through direct, personal experience. This long journey was appropriate for my learning—and unlearning—as well as for my healing, and it is simply being shared with those who may be curious about another seeker's experience. Ultimately, your journey—each person's journey—is unique because each person is a unique expression of Life.

More and more people are sensing that a shift is happening on the planet at this time, and it is happening very rapidly. So it is understandable that our needs, questions, perceptions, learning, experiences, beliefs, knowledge and understanding are shifting right along with it. People of all ages, including the young and those who have never opened a spiritual book in their lives are jumping in, each with their own outlook on life and the world, each with their own soul's unique experiences. And that is exactly what this shift is about: new perspectives, new knowledge, new understanding, and new experiences. It's not about dusting off the old and producing a nicer version or a more modern version of the old. It is now time for a radically new experience for humanity—the key here being "new," an experience that is completely different from and beyond anything we have ever known before on Earth.

Although my work presents a perspective based on over half a century of study and experience in the fields of astrology, numerology and various spiritual teachings, it is by far not the only perspective. It is simply one way of examining and attempting to understand how this shift is unfolding, based on one person's experience. Ultimately, each person's journey will generate an inimitable and equally valid perspective, but more importantly, one that is appropriate for them, a fact that is completely in alignment with the nature of the Age of Aquarius.

Many people today are familiar with their Sun sign or perhaps even their astrology chart; however, there is no need to know much or even anything at all about astrology to read this book. The astrological perspective is explained in simple terms—hopefully—and basically serves as a backdrop for shedding light and clearing the path as we transition from one two-thousand-year period to the next, or from the Age of Pisces into the Age of Aquarius. The reader will no doubt recognize some of the core patterns inherent in the astrological Eras mentioned in this work as they reflect characteristics, traits, events, stories and trends found in our history over many millennia.

Given my experience in the field, I have found that the astrological backdrop provides a clearer understanding of what is occurring on Earth at this time. With the tremendous amount of information exploding in our world today, each must find that which will be most helpful given their unique language, experience, knowledge and level of awareness. From my perspective, a study of the astrological Eras has provided invaluable insights as to how we can move forward and bring about the much-needed change on

Earth with grace and with as few delays, challenges and obstacles as possible.

In my last book, *Aquarius: The Age of Revelation, Choice and Transformation* (AARCT), the journey of humanity over the last 6000 years was examined against the backdrop of the Eras of Taurus, Aries and Pisces. This journey was then presented as a way of identifying the potential impact of our past as it is carried forward into the newly emerging Era of Aquarius. In this book, we will focus mostly on the nature of Aquarius, the challenges that are likely to be encountered, and how to transition into this new Age in the most pain-free, and effective way possible. We will further explore how, during this critical period of transition, we will have the opportunity, if we so choose, to raise human consciousness and ultimately, the entire earthly experience to a whole new level.

As mentioned in AARCT, while history is not my forte, it is important to be aware of certain past events and trends, as many of these remain deeply entrenched in our beliefs and cultures. Some of these are then carried forward into the newly emerging Era, and may interfere with our progress. By being aware of past decisions and choices, we can more easily avoid repeating the same mistakes. Properly informed, we will be better equipped to correct and release what is no longer needed or desired. Then we can begin to introduce approaches that are in harmony with the energies of the new Era and are in line with the new Earth we wish to create. Some of the main themes introduced in AARCT will be further developed in this book as we explore the best ways to heal ourselves and release our past so we can more easily rise to a higher, richer experience for all life on Earth.

If I had any concerns about sharing my weird experiences in my writing, I received confirmation in the monthly message from Archangel Michael as transmitted by Ronna Herman:

> Many of you are experiencing miraculous events in your lives, and we ask you to be bold enough to share these wonders with your friends. Do not fear ridicule or criticism.

You will find approval more often than disapproval and interest more often than disdain.

I couldn't help but say yes, okay, let's do it. I will write about these experiences; some will resonate with them, and others won't, and that's okay. I'm just doing my job. Thank you for the support.

Book Recap

The books in this series represent a lifelong search for the true meaning of life. Each book describes a unique stage on this journey, exploring teachings and eventually revelations that provided new perspectives and understanding. For those curious about these earlier works, the following is a brief recap of their general content.

Making Peace with God covers the early years of my quest, leading up to the life-altering discovery of *A Course in Miracles*. I was then introduced to the works of Course teacher Kenneth Wapnick, and Gary Renard, author of *The Disappearance of the Universe*, which were helpful for understanding what was for me a very complex work.

Leaving the Desert is an in-depth exploration of what became for me a very important teaching, *A Course in Miracles*. As a devoted Course student, I was determined to learn everything I could from this work so that I could effectively put it into practice in my everyday life.

In *Choosing the Miracle*, the journey continues, but with the addition of the helpful perspective from the Raj materials, as channelled by Paul Tuttle. It includes insights received from Jesus as I began to learn how to connect with guidance.

The Movement of Being is a more personal work, and includes much guidance from my new best friend Jesus. It focuses on how to apply these teachings in everyday life, from how to be in a body to how to interact with others. It answers many questions about how to engage in this transition to a new way of Being.

The Healing of Humanity presents what has been shared in the previous books in a way that might be more suitable for the current generation, in a way that is less spiritual, religious or New Agey. For this reason, I referred to my guide Jesus as my Friend, and the general language was toned down a little bit to sound less spiritual.

In *Aquarius: The Age of Revelation, Choice and Transformation* the recent teachings being made available to humanity are placed against the background of the transition between the Eras of Pisces and Aquarius. It sheds light on the challenges and opportunities of this time, so we can make the most appropriate choices for ourselves and the world.

CHAPTER 1

The First Step

Love will enter immediately into ANY mind which truly wants it, but it MUST want it truly. (ACIM, Ch. 4, p. 77)

Interesting Times

While I have accepted writing as an integral part of my purpose in this life, I'm really a practical, hands-on, experience-based person. So words, at least in and of themselves are not necessarily my primary focus—except, of course, when I'm writing a book, which involves lots of rewriting. Lots! For those familiar with my astrology book, *Astrological Crosses*, this might make sense, given that I have only one planet in a mutable sign, Mars—totally action-based— which happens to be in Sagittarius, a fire sign, adding more fuel to the action. I actually work at a sit-stand desk where I dictate and reread my text aloud—so very Mars in Sag! Nonetheless, as we will see in later chapters, words do play an important role in our lives, perhaps far more than we realize. At some point it can be helpful and may even be necessary to take a closer look at the words we use, especially the ones we cling to, for the meaning they hold has a significant correlation with how we see and experience ourselves and the world.

Given that particular planetary configuration in my natal chart, it is easy to understand why I would find experimenting with a new recipe in the kitchen to be more fun than sitting at a computer writing words, which is exactly what I did while in the middle of editing this chapter. Oh, and by the way, the adzuki bean tempeh experiment turned out really well! Okay, back to writing. So it is that writing isn't easy for yours truly, at least not the first draft. I guess it's the rewriting part I like best, because by then, I know what to write about, Mars in Sag kicks in, and I get to experiment and play around with the words until I get a feeling for them. Then it becomes a dynamic experience and so, definitely, the rewriting part is more enjoyable. In the new energy of Aquarius, the experience—first-hand, direct, personal experience—will be among the most important means of learning, growing and expanding into and embodying a new way of Being for humanity.

Having taken a few months break from writing after the publication of AARCT in the summer of 2021, I was eager to work on the next book, but had no first draft to play with. The problem was that I simply didn't know where to start. I had continued to gather tidbits of notes, guidance and inspiration in my journal. Actually, I had gathered over 60,000 words. Still, I could not see clearly what more could be said about the shift into the new Era—the Golden Age, the Galactic Age, or whatever name it is being given—now facing humanity.

What was clear was that from our current human perspective on Earth, we are facing a totally new Era, with a new energy, something with which we are not familiar. Even if we have experienced a similar Era in some far distant past, given our present limited, linear-thinking, 3-D conditioning, except for perhaps a very few rare souls, we have no memory of such an experience. More importantly, even if we were to remember the past, nothing says that it must or even will—or should—be repeated. So, if we truly long for something new, if we do not want to repeat old, worn-out, untenable patterns, we must be ready to accept and embrace being in a radically different, totally new way. This fact alone will be a challenge, at least for a time, or at least until we begin to reap some of the benefits of being in this new way through first-hand, direct experience.

I also wondered how I could write about experiences and insights gathered over a lifelong quest that, from my perspective, seemed difficult to put into words. For example, at a very young age I had

CHAPTER 1 · THE FIRST STEP

experiences that I never shared with anyone. When I was about four years old, during what was supposed to be afternoon naptime, I would rise up out of my body and "fly" outside, where I would hover above the house and then venture on down the street. Thrilled by the experience, I would fly back home and go find my mother in the kitchen, her favourite spot in the house. Floating up near the ceiling, I would then invite her to join me: "Viens, Maman, c'est facile!" I remember those words so clearly, spoken in French, my mother tongue, as well as the joy and excitement I felt as I invited her to come up and join me. I didn't question the experience; it seemed so easy and natural. It was just a normal thing to do. But she never saw me; never even heard me.

And then, as shared in *Making Peace with God* (MPG), there was my deep curiosity about God. Who was God? Where was God? I wanted to meet Him, to know Him, to talk with Him.

> I recall when I was around eight or nine years old, lying in bed late at night, unable to fall asleep, pondering the nature of God. I don't remember how long these late night musings lasted, perhaps weeks or months, only that they were very real to me at the time. They would occur after everyone had fallen asleep. The house was silent. Wide awake, I would let my mind wander out to the end of the universe, imagining myself flying through space, beyond the stars and the galaxies, to the other side of infinity. It didn't seem to matter that we had been taught that infinity went on and on forever and ever; for me, infinity had to end somewhere because where infinity ended, God began. In fact, the eternity issue was a bit bothersome to me, for, if God was eternal and living in eternity and He had made us in his image and likeness, how come our universe was outside of God? Why was He so far away?

> While moving through space on my nightly voyages, I would hear a strange, high-pitched sound, not unpleasant to the ear, but definitely unlike anything I would ever hear in the regular world. The sound would accompany me, rising in

intensity, as I travelled away from my bed, far from my home and city, further and further up through the blackness of the night sky, past the solar system, beyond the tiny white lights of the stars. When I reached what I thought must be the edge of the universe, where God lived, I stopped. Standing there, alone, feeling at peace, I waited for God. Although I couldn't see Him, I knew He must be there, somewhere. He just couldn't come and see me at that moment. He must be very busy, I told myself. Besides, there was no hurry. I was young and there was plenty of time before I would return home. There was simply no doubt in my mind that He was there. Standing patiently at the threshold of God's home, I believed that one day He would answer me and I would be welcomed home.

One night, I told myself that perhaps it wasn't such a great idea to wander so far out into the universe like that. It occurred to me that perhaps I should be afraid. Although I had not once felt the slightest twinge of fear as I stood by the gates of the home of God, I managed to convince myself that I should be afraid. That night, I went to my parents' room and crawled into bed next to my mother. She told me that I was too old to sleep in her bed. I told her I'd had a bad dream, although I knew very well that I hadn't and that there was really nothing to fear. I stayed there a minute, maybe two. Not feeling particularly comforted from my imagined non-fear, I decided to return to my room. After that night, my late night visits with God came to an end. (MPG, Ch. 2, p. 22)

These are not experiences I shared with anyone when I was young, which is a good thing, because in those days they probably would have locked me up in an institution and thrown away the key. However, I have no doubt that many young souls on Earth have had similar experiences, and many more are likely having similar, even more far-reaching experiences today. The question now is: are we listening to their stories? Are we ready to support and encourage them in their quest to experience what lies beyond history, culture, convention and tradition? Are we willing to set aside what we think we know so we may help them journey beyond the known?

Fortunately, much has changed over the last few decades. Having entered and fully embraced the "information age," there is no shortage of unique, unusual and sometimes even mind-blowing stories, perspectives and experiences being shared today. In these changing times, many souls are speaking out and sharing their stories, some of which are helping humanity come together and move forward to a new experience on Earth. The challenge now is to be able to sort through this overwhelming amount of information and decide what is and what is not relevant and helpful for us—a very important key point during this time of transition.

Back to the present day, facing the writing of yet another book, I was well aware that whatever I would write needed to be written in everyday, practical, relatable language. In other words, as a lifelong spiritual seeker, the unusual perspectives that were coming to me needed to be conveyed, as much as possible, in non-religious, minimally spiritual, even non-new-agey, twenty-first-century language. Such was the style suitable for the new Era of Aquarius. There is now no doubt in my mind that this is the reason why I was born with the Moon and ascendant in Aquarius. I get it; but above all, I feel it. And so I simply trusted that as I gained more relevant life experiences, the words would come and I would know what to write and, hopefully, how to write it.

> The history of man in the world as he sees it has not yet been marked by any genuine or comprehensive reawakening or rebirth. (ACIM, Ch. 2, p. 22)

Dipping into the Past

Before undertaking this daunting task, I took a little timeout from writing about our path forward to take stock of our history and its impact on the current state of the world. I researched a broad range of subjects from spirituality and religion to geopolitics, ancient history, archaeology, and the increasingly popular topic of extraterrestrial or alien phenomena. I read books, watched videos and listened to talks by those considered to be experts in their fields. In the end, while this research was helpful, it was more daunting than actual writing. Digging into the history of humanity quickly became overwhelming, and I would soon learn why this was so. What was first made crystal clear is that change is needed now, very much so, because we certainly do not want a repeat of our history, nor do we want just a fancy, hi-tech version of the past.

To be honest, the state of the world or world events in general, is not something I had dwelled on much throughout my life. For the most part, as a single mom, I had been focused on raising my children, building my consulting practice, paying the bills, working with clients and, when there was time, a little bit of writing. We did not even have cable television when I was growing up, nor when I was raising my children. In fact, for many years, we didn't even have a television. I had always been more interested in the deeper, self-discovery and healing aspects of life rather than the material, mundane, economic, social or political happenings of the world. Plus, I had, and still have, a very, very low tolerance for drama. So, whatever was going on "out there" had never played a major role in my life, at least not until recent years.

As we now find ourselves living in a time of significant change tainted by ever-increasing levels of drama, I thought it was important to be at least minimally informed. However, in my deep dive into our history and its bearing on current events, I eventually reached a point where I had taken in too much dark, dramatic, conflicting and contradictory information. I simply threw up my hands and declared, "No more!" Given what I had been learning, I almost regretted having opened that door. It was as though I had removed the lid from a huge garbage can—one that just got bigger and bigger the more I explored its contents. I needed to get my head out of there. The expression "may you live in interesting times" now seemed like an understatement, or perhaps even a curse. Ignorance is bliss, as they say; but, is it helpful?

CHAPTER 1 · THE FIRST STEP

While some of what I learned was uplifting and inspiring—actually, very little was uplifting or inspiring—much more was deeply disturbing. It was like watching a dark science fiction drama series. There was information that actually stirred deep anger and resentment. This was especially the case with the stories of interventions and genetic manipulation of humans in ancient times by supposedly "higher" or "more advanced" beings, in particular, the beings mere mortals would come to label as "gods." If they had been so highly evolved, how could they justifiably perform such heinous acts? At one point, it felt very personal, as though I had been there and suffered great loss, hence the reason for my anger and resentment.

That deep dive into our history led to moments of utter hopelessness and despair, leaving me with more questions than answers. What was it all for? Why bother? What can I do about it? Is there actually anything I can do about it? What am I here for? Or better yet, why am I here? These are questions asked by millions of people around the world at this time, and I wholeheartedly related. In order to get back on my journey and return to that quiet, centred place of Being, I eventually saw that all that was needed was to forgive and release. To continue on this journey, above all else, I needed to be free. Holding on to the past, no matter how tragic or horrendous, or even no matter how accurate, would prevent me from moving forward. One thing was absolutely clear: I wanted to move forward. The key here was to let it all go—just let it all go. We cannot climb that hill to a higher level of awareness if we are carrying a trunk full of ancient baggage. It is imperative that we let it all go.

This was not the first time I had gone down that rabbit hole. I had experienced a similar process of diving into history and current world events in preparation for the writing of AARCT, a process that had also led to a most uncomfortable detour into darkness. You'd think that I had learned from that experience but, while I had gained knowledge about our history, apparently I had not learned the right lesson. Interestingly, this time around I learned that it was the fact that I had reacted to the information revealed during those deep dives that was significant. The information itself was not the issue. My responses, my reactions, my perceptions and how the information made me feel—my anger and resentment—were what truly mattered.

As Jeshua (or Jesus, if you prefer) tells us in *A Course in Miracles* and in *The Way of the Heart* (WOH):

I have no neutral thoughts. (ACIM, Lesson 16)
Listen well and carefully: *All events are neutral. You* are the one that places the value upon it. (WOH, Lesson 9)

This jarring realization had a profound impact on how I would see the world and how I would experience myself from that point forward. While it is clear that no matter how enlightened, educated, informed or self-aware we may be, we cannot simply go out and change the world according to our desire or our will, no matter how well-intentioned. Accepting responsibility for how we see the world, in fact, for all of our thoughts, actions, reactions and responses, will be an essential part of the process as we step through the Gateway into the new Era for humankind. Once this has been understood, we are more likely to know how to proceed, whether or not to take action, and how we can best contribute to the healing of humanity.

In the end, I concluded that I would get what I needed from more reliable sources: my inner voice and my Guides. Then, I would write from knowledge that naturally comes from first-hand personal experience. This is the perspective that is most helpful for me and, from what I am seeing this is also the case for a growing number of souls experiencing life on Earth at this time. So let us learn what is needed so we can move forward and create a new world with grace, love, wisdom, and with as much ease as possible. What will this shift mean for us individually, for all of humanity and for planet Earth? How can we make the transition as smooth and easy as possible?

CHAPTER 1 • THE FIRST STEP

Where Peace Begins

Before moving forward with the main topics of this book, I was nudged to share a story, actually, one of the stories that drove me back to writing after several months delay. I had been pondering the subject of war, something that had troubled me deeply after having experienced a brief past-life flash of a soldier. There stood a young African American man holding up a rifle having to make the most difficult decision of his life. Should he pull the trigger or should he put down the gun? He had hoped to do right by his impoverished family, as well as serve his country by joining the military. However, rather than giving him a sense of worth and pride, this experience caused him profound confusion and an overwhelming sense of personal failure.

Feeling deeply conflicted, the soldier had not been able to carry out his duty. Instead, he laid down his gun and walked off the field. In so doing, while honouring God's commandment—Thou shalt not kill!—he had failed his country and, above all, his family, who depended on him for financial support. While I have no way of knowing for certain if this was my past life, it explained why I could never watch war movies. It also explained why, half a century ago, while my brother was playing Chopin on the piano and my father was playing Segovia and Montoya on the guitar, I was attracted to jazz and blues styles of music that were not played on mainstream radio nor in my home at the time. Hearing that blues harp (harmonica) still rips me apart.

Another item I picked up from that flash was my tendency for bailing in this lifetime. I had worked in many jobs, studied a wide range of subjects, had my share of failed relationships—always bailing and moving on, bailing and moving on. For that pattern, I had felt shame and guilt. This constant bailing had prevented me from being successful in any particular field. However, my Guides stepped in and assured me that I should not feel that way since my varied experiences had been most helpful in my work with clients. I could better understand them, I could relate to them because I had been there and done that. So bailing was not necessarily a bad thing. It was just a matter of making a different choice and moving on. For that reassurance I was most grateful.

For the reader not familiar with my previous books, note that "my Guides" or as I sometimes call them "my Friends" are those who are helping me on this journey. Since a very young age, I had felt a connection with Jeshua and Mother Mary. Many snippets of guidance were shared in my books, for which I was deeply grateful as I struggled through the challenging teaching of *A Course in Miracles*. Since then, several more have been added to the group. I don't know their names, nor how many there are, but I sense their presence. Plus, this help is coming from dimensions that are beyond our familiar 3-D level, so this may not be fully understandable at this time. Receiving guidance is not something unique as we are all receiving help, especially during this time of great change. In fact, help has always been available. Everyone has experienced a moment where they reached up and thanked "God" for helping them with a seemingly impossible situation. As we want more help, all that is needed is to be open to the idea that there are souls residing beyond the physical dimension—kind, compassionate, understanding, loving souls who remain always available to help us. Okay, let's return to the topic at hand.

While doing research for my last book, I spent a fair amount of time combing through the *Timetables of History*. It was disheartening to discover that, over the past 6000 years of recorded history, there were but a few years during which there were no wars or battles of any kind on Earth. In an attempt to process the reality of war, how war seems to be the only way to resolve conflict, how we honour our war heroes for their service and ultimately their sacrifices, how billions of dollars are spent on developing and manufacturing increasingly powerful weapons, it came to me that war was almost inevitable in the current state of the human condition. In fact, war is, in a way, almost normal or even natural, given that it is nothing more than an amplified or larger version of what occurs in everyday life. Conflict of some kind is almost

CHAPTER 1 • THE FIRST STEP

inevitable in a consciousness infused with a deep-seated culture of duality and separation.

Again, what was needed was to forgive and let it all go. This was simply an aspect—one aspect—of the human experience and it should not be judged, feared, criticized, demeaned, hated or condemned. Then, if I was able to forgive, I would return to the only place that mattered: my heart, the single most important key to breaking free of the old and moving forward into the new experience of Being. Also, I realized that forgiveness was really for me, not for anyone or anything outside myself, and so I began to forgive and let it all go. Almost instantly, I was overwhelmed by a deep feeling of liberation and freedom, but above all, a swelling in my heart.

After helping a neighbour prepare photos for a calendar she would give to her sister as a Christmas gift, she suggested that I create one for my mom. At first I thought it would be too much work—digging out and scanning old photos, modifying resolutions, cropping images, refreshing colours—but in the end, I decided, sure, why not. Besides, it would be fun. Maybe I would find some nice photos I had developed in my darkroom ages ago.

The project turned out to be far more difficult than anticipated. It wasn't the photo edits that were difficult, but rather the heart-wrenching realization that war existed in my family. I had pulled out a photo of me and my two brothers on a family vacation, standing by the lake, huddled next to each other in the cool, fresh air. Lac Saint Jean—the place of my birth—has always held a special place in my heart, as it is one of the most beautiful places I have known. Looking at the picture of the three of us smiling and standing so close to each other, I couldn't hold back the tears. It had been years since my brothers and I had stood in the same room, let alone spoken to each other. Over time, the cancer of divisiveness had found its way into my family, spreading out to other family members. There was war at home, right here in my family and, as shared by so many of my friends and clients, this was not an uncommon situation.

Sadly, this was no different from what was going on around the world on a larger scale. How can we expect to have peace on Earth when war has taken root in our families? After all, we are the world! We must stop and take matters in hand, now, once and for all. The truth is that peace begins at home. We need to do something now! Fortunately, the good news is that we can do something now, but the choice remains ours to make, and this is another key—we always have the freedom to choose. What choices will we make as we move forward into this new Age? Will we have the courage to choose peace? Or will we continue to find a sense of righteous vindication through our constant battles and wars? Isn't it time for real change? Do we have what it takes to create a truly new world?

Standing at a Crossroads

Clearly, there is no arguing the fact that humanity is—that we are, right here, right now—standing at a crossroads with many potential avenues before us. How we will proceed from this point forward is what is important, even critical, at this time. As an astrologer, I refer to this period as the transition between the Ages of Pisces and Aquarius, a most significant time of transition for humanity. As we will see, this is a transition between two fundamentally different Eras, or seasons, as I like to describe them. Even without the astrological perspective, very few would dispute the fact that we are at a crossroads, and from what we can gather, change is needed—very much needed! The fact is that the transition into the new energies has begun. While many still do not understand that great transformation is underway, whether we like it or not, there is no going back to the way things were. This is good news, although some will not see it that way and may even do whatever it takes to put a halt to this transition. As always, each person remains free to choose which direction they will take.

How can we move forward and consider, let alone embrace, a new Era in a time that seems more confusing, disturbing, frightening, uprooting and challenging than ever? More importantly, are we actually capable of moving forward? Do we have what it takes?

CHAPTER 1 · THE FIRST STEP

Are we ready to let go of the old and embrace the new? How much of the old are we willing to release? How much new are we willing to embrace? Or, will we continue down the same old beaten path travelled by our ancestors—travelled by us in past lives—only now, with fancier technology? Do we have it in our hearts to welcome and bring about this much-needed change with courage, grace, patience, harmony, compassion and wisdom?

As a collective, or family of beings, we now find ourselves standing on ancient territory, built up over thousands and thousands of years. We have learned much, experienced much and developed much, but we have also acquired and developed habits and behaviours that may not represent our highest potential, or may not reflect our most enlightened expression. During this transition phase, we have the opportunity to make significant, deeply altering changes. We can always attempt to work with the old broken bits and pieces, clean them up, dust them off, and rearrange them in the hope of creating a better world for ourselves. However, by using the old bits and pieces, the best we can hope for is a patched up, rearranged version of the old. This will not likely bring about the new world or the new experiences that so many are now calling for, at least not in the near future.

Alternatively, we can discard the old, step forward onto new, clean, uncharted territory, connect with a higher aspect of ourselves, claim our power and create a brand-new experience for the human collective. Whereas this option holds the most potential for the greatest transformation and the highest possible expression for all life on Earth, it will require a bit more work—okay, maybe a lot more work—especially on the part of those individuals who have the courage to actively engage in the transformation while it is still in its stage of infancy. This is a choice that each person will need to make for themselves. Most likely, we will proceed somewhere between the two alternatives: by attempting to fix some of the old while tentatively stepping forward into the new.

There are many souls who have already declared their desire to create a new world for humanity, and many souls who are returning to Earth now are here to contribute to the creation of this new world. However, there are those who will want to rebuild with the old bits and pieces, those who will not be interested in a new world, or a new way of being on Earth, since they have various vested interests in the old structures. And that's okay. We do not need to worry about those souls. Somewhere in the universe, there will be a place for them to continue their experience, should they so choose. But most likely, once they catch a glimpse of the wonderful potential emerging in this new way of life on Earth, they may very well decide to join in. One of our greatest contributions will be to show them how it's done, by our example of living in a new way. Each one has a role to play, and not one is greater than another.

What we are more concerned with at this time, at least those who are ready to create a new world, is how to go about this transition in the smoothest, least painful, most effective and actually most enjoyable and fascinating way possible. The question each individual needs to ask themselves is: do I want to rebuild the old, or do I want something completely new? Your answer to this question will determine your path forward during this transition phase. Here we encounter another key point: this journey is about you, it's about me, and it's about each and every unique life expression on Earth. And so, all that is needed is for each one to focus on his or her own journey. That's it. Nothing more complicated than that. Well, except for a few long-held, built-in obstacles, which we will examine more closely in later chapters.

The Single Most Important Ingredient

As shared in AARCT and *The Healing of Humanity*, it wasn't until I had reached the ripe old age of 58 that I first experienced, or actually just felt love for myself—true love, that is. No, that's not a typo—58! Better late than never, right? But that's okay, because it gave me the opportunity to know what true self-love felt like in contrast with the sense of deep inner longing that is experienced when true love is, for whatever reason, not experienced.

CHAPTER 1 • THE FIRST STEP

One day, I was reading a section in one of my books that a wonderful soul had graciously offered to translate into French. Rereading my work, once published, is not something that I normally did, probably out of fear of finding errors of some kind. But that day, as I was reading a paragraph in *Choosing the Miracle*, all of a sudden, out of nowhere, I felt a deep, warm flash: "I loved that author. Wow! That author was me! I had just loved me! Then I realized that I had never, in my entire life, even for one minute, experienced love for myself." (AARCT, Ch. 5, p. 74) Huh! What a mind-blowing realization!

Oh, I had loved my daughters deeply, totally, unconditionally. I would have done anything for them. However, I had never felt that same kind of love for myself. Then it occurred to me that I had deprived them of a very important lesson. Imagine the ambivalence of the young child who is loved unconditionally by a parent, but that parent has never truly loved himself or herself in the same way. Like most people, I had felt satisfaction and pride for some of my accomplishments, gratitude for the many gifts that life had offered me, but I had never truly felt love for me. What a revelation! This was indeed an important revelation; no, it was the single most important revelation of my entire life! In fact, I don't recall ever having been taught to love myself, ever. Actually, self-love was equated more with arrogance and pride; therefore it was not openly encouraged as it was even considered a sin. Imagine that!

Shaken by this unbelievable revelation, I was curious to know if I was the only person on Earth who had never really loved herself/himself. So I asked some of my clients if they had ever truly loved themselves.

> Most had no problem sharing how well they had fared despite the obstacles and challenges they had encountered during their life. Some pointed out their accomplishments and worldly successes, expressing how happy and grateful and pleased they were. Everyone has given their story that positive spin, at least once or twice in their life, despite the fact that this is not quite how they felt inside.

Not really getting the response I was looking for, I would ask the question again, but with a little twist. Do you remember how you felt the day your son or daughter was born? If they had no children, I asked about their puppy or kitten or horse—whatever they had loved in their life. To illustrate the point, I would fold my arms across my chest and hug myself. Again, I would ask: How did you feel when you held your baby girl or baby boy that first time?

Then would come a smile, a sigh, an aha, an expression of sweet tenderness, raised eyebrows or an almost breathless pause. Of course, it felt wonderful. Once they truly understood—and felt—what I meant, I would follow up with the next big question. Have you ever felt that way about yourself? Oh, you mean, have I ever felt that kind of love for me? After another pause, perhaps a quick breath, maybe a cringe, sometimes teary-eyed, astonished by the sudden revelation, there might be a shrug, a slow shake of the head, and the admission to never having truly ever done so. Of all the people I asked, only one could honestly say that she had felt that kind of unconditional love for herself. To this day, I remain surprised at how rare these precious experiences of true self-love are. (AARCT, Ch. 5, pp. 74-75)

Given what I now know and understand about the human condition, I am no longer taken aback by the absence of true self-love in the world at this time, as well as throughout history. Fortunately, I have also discovered how easy it is to have this experience. But more than that, it has become clear that self-love will be a crucial element as we move forward into a new experience for humanity. Therefore it is not surprising to see the growing number of references to "self-care" or being "heart-centred" in books and teachings today, something that is indeed very much needed, actually something that has been overlooked and even rebuked as an act of arrogance or selfishness for millennia.

While curiosity, a desire to experience something different—something truly new—and the courage to explore the unknown

CHAPTER 1 · THE FIRST STEP

are essential requirements for making a smooth transition into the new Era, the single, most important ingredient is—and always has been—Love. If we are unable to be from that heart-centred place, we will not be able to forgive, release the old and be free to claim a new experience for ourselves and for all of humanity. Without love, divisiveness, inequality, competition, fear and war cannot be set aside. As we come to know love for ourselves, it will become easy, even natural, to know love for our brothers and sisters, no matter how undeserving they may seem. To love is natural because it is an inherent aspect of our true Being as expressions of the One Source, and so it is the most important ingredient for our collective healing.

Love is essentially the key to the Gateway that leads to that greater experience of Being—the ultimate experience that each and every one of us so longs for. In the Age of Aquarius—an Era in tune with deep feeling—it does not take long to realize that love feels so much greater than anything else that can be experienced in the human condition. It is the one aspect of life that is clearly beyond the basic physical-material experience. But, as *A Course in Miracles* says, the meaning of love is not something that can be taught. Love cannot be understood; it must be experienced. Fortunately, first-hand experience is an essential trait of Aquarius.

We now need to understand how we came to this place of inability to know love for ourselves, for each other, for all life forms, as well as for our home planet Earth. This is an essential step, one that each person needs to take for themselves, but it may not be easy to take, at least not at first. In order for this to happen, whatever stands in the way of that love must be brought to light and then released. Only then can we begin to have that experience of love we so very much yearn for. Once the way is made clear, the miracle happens and love simply flows because love is at the heart of each one's Being. In so doing, we will be ready to move forward into the unknown, into a completely new Era for all life on Earth, an Era of love, respect, creativity, discovery, wisdom, beauty, compassion, harmony, inclusiveness, equality and fairness.

Are you ready to take this step? If so, take a deep breath, clear your mind of all thoughts; go to that quiet place within. Seek out that inner child, the one who feels alone, who is sometimes, even oftentimes, fearful—the one who is so much in need of love. Now, wrap your arms around yourself and give yourself a big hug. Feel that warm love for the child inside, the one who was bold enough, courageous enough to step into this experience on Earth at this challenging time of transition and change. Give yourself the gift of love, that one gift that is more important than anything else in the entire universe. Breathe, feel yourself enveloped, safe, warm and filled with love.

Now that you have become familiar with this feeling of True Love, take it outside. While on your way to work, or grocery shopping, or just out for a walk, if you spot someone who appears to be in need of love—and who isn't in need of love!—imagine a wave of love pouring out from your heart washing over them and enveloping them with that most glorious feeling. You don't even need to look at them, as you don't want to make them feel uncomfortable. Look away and just let that Love flow. This is easy to do with strangers, as there is no history that stands in the way. In time, this simple practice will help heal those special relationships with family and friends, those relationships tainted with history and memory.

My preferred writing time is early morning. I get dressed, water my microgreens, grab my breakfast and head for the computer. I also make sure to grab my recorder since very often insights about writing are received just as I am about to get up in the morning. Lately, I noticed that when I get some weird ideas for my writing, confirmation or clarification often comes in some form of coincidence, or synchronicity. This happens especially when I'm questioning how to write or how to develop a topic that may not necessarily be easy to convey in everyday language. So, I was not surprised when I checked my morning email and read the daily message from Jeshua, as channelled by Judith Coates. I usually find these daily messages uplifting and inspiring, and so they are a great way to start the day. However, while working on this book, several of these messages were so much in line with what I was writing that I would shake my head and chuckle. I know that we are not alone, and we are receiving help from those loving souls who are answering our calls. Thank you. Thank you. Thank you.

> The Love of true friendship is all that you can ever offer another one, and it is the grandest of gifts, to give of your Self—capital "S"—and in the giving, guess what happens? You find your Self. You experience your Self. As you allow the heart to open and to love freely, caring, understanding, asking to be companion upon the path, as you allow the shutters of the heart to be flung wide open you find your Self and you experience the Love that you have been searching for. (Jeshua Online—Daily Message)

CHAPTER 2

Our Place in the Cosmos

Ancient Egyptians considered cosmic life to exist harmoniously and synchronically with mortal life, only separated by the veil of materiality. There were no separate disciplines of astronomy and astrology as there are now, but they interacted with each other in a system that emphasized these intricately related powers, visible and invisible. (*Ancient Origins of the Zodiac*, Ezra Ivanov)

The Choice for Peace

At a gathering in a neighbour's condo over the 2022 holidays, a couple of exclamations and raised eyebrows were expressed when someone mentioned that I was an astrologer and an expert in numerology. "Ah, you're a psychic, you're a clairvoyant!" one lady said, as though I had some sort of magical, fortune-telling superpower. I just smiled and said nothing, as this was not the first time I had encountered such reactions regarding my lifelong career path. Another participant eagerly chimed in, acknowledging that this was true and the chatter simply moved on to other topics. Sometimes it's best to not say anything unless a question has been asked and it is one for which I have a helpful and appropriate answer.

A few years earlier, I had accompanied a friend to a meeting of amateur astronomers. Given the likelihood that the mere mention of the word "astrology" might stir up a bit of controversy—in fact I was quite certain that it would—I asked that she refrain from bringing up the subject. Not surprisingly, about halfway through what had been a calm, casual evening of chatting about black holes, solar flares, and other popular astronomy topics, she asked for their thoughts on astrology. Since Libras find it hard to resist—and actually thoroughly enjoy—a good debate, and my friend is a Libra, I should have known better. I should also add that I have two planets in Libra, including its ruler Venus, along with three planets in the seventh house, Libra's natural home. So I guess I too like a bit of debate—maybe just a hint. Once the cat was out of the bag, an animated discussion erupted on the unscientific foundation and inconsistencies of astrology, basically attacking a body of knowledge I had acquired over 50 years of study, research and practice.

I was able to calmly refrain from expressing my views until one participant stood up and began to pace slowly in front of us. He appeared pensive, perhaps a bit authoritative, as though looking for the right words. Hands clasped behind his back and head held high, finally, he proclaimed that astrology was a sickness. At that point, the Libra in me could no longer remain quiet. With great restraint, feigning simple curiosity I asked him if he could name some of the books he had studied, pointing out that as a serious researcher, his opinion must have been based on first-hand knowledge and valid studies. The lack of response to my question indicated that his opinion was in fact unfounded, at which point he left the conversation, and quietly walked to the other end of the hall.

The discussion did continue for a while, with references limited to horoscopes and sun-sign astrology. By all accounts, none of the other participants had studied the subject. More importantly, there appeared to be no interest in learning more, since questions that might have shed light on the subject were never asked. The consensus was that, given the absence of scientific validation, astrology was nothing more than a foolish fantasy. Given the clear lack of interest, I remained quiet.

The circumstances of that evening came to mind several times over the following days, understandably eliciting some disquiet. While I might have been justified in feeling a certain smug self-satisfaction with the position I had taken, instead, I felt unease. At first, I was troubled by how, in a comfortable suburban setting, a group of intelligent, educated individuals could express such a lack of openness to what was simply a different perspective on a subject about which they had no knowledge. How was humanity ever to find healing when, in seemingly friendly, peaceful surroundings, such forms of trivial divisiveness still managed to reign supreme.

On closer examination, it didn't take long for me to see that the real reason for the disquiet was that I had not exercised sufficient vigilance with regard to my mind. It's never about the other person; I knew that. I had effectively abandoned my peace, even if only briefly, thereby depriving myself of being from my centre, the only place from which a situation can be addressed with true intelligence and wisdom, but above all, with loving acceptance. I knew better, yet, I had allowed myself to indulge in a bit of divisive, self-gratifying banter, which I paid for with a case of disquiet. This was actually an example of the denial of one of our true superpowers: the ability and the freedom to stand back, breathe and choose for peace, regardless of the situation, even a seemingly insignificant one.

I reminded myself that each person is making his or her own way to the truth, one tiny step, or misstep, at a time. Whether or not we are in accord with those steps, we must be in accord with the soul taking the steps. That is where true Oneness lies, and so it is where true healing begins. Hope lies not in agreeing on the steps, but rather in seeing and being with the one on the journey, and then helping or supporting them in any way we can. My job was not to convince them of the validity of my work, nor to expect them to open their minds and look beyond their telescopes. My job was to see the One in them and by extension, experience Oneness within myself. Only then could I express what the world needs most: the releasing of boundaries and divisiveness through loving acceptance.

The Gift of Curiosity

Despite having easy access to abundant information today—sometimes it seems like an overabundance—many people still have no clue as to what astrology actually is, let alone how it works. This should probably be of no surprise since in order to gain even a basic understanding of the subject—of any subject, for that matter—a bit of actual study and perhaps some practical application is required. Just as you would learn more about physiology and anatomy by reading the classic text *Gray's Anatomy* rather than by watching the television series *Grey's Anatomy*, you would learn more about astrology by studying reputable textbooks rather than by reading daily horoscopes.

It is not the purpose of this book to explain how astrology works, or to explore its very long history. That would require a lifetime of research, and even then, there may not even be a consensus on the question of its true genesis. Besides, the focus of interest of this work is more on understanding the nature of the current transition and uncovering how to best navigate it. Nonetheless, a brief look into the origins of astrology can be not only informative but also quite fascinating since there is far more to its history than is generally known. It also sheds light on how information is carried forward as well as how it can also be left behind.

As recent research and studies in ancient history and archaeology have uncovered, astrology and astronomy were once intimately connected. These studies show that long ago, there was an openness to the idea that there exists an inherent correlation between all aspects of creation, from the known to the unknown. This concept of an intrinsic unity in the field of creation is a popular topic of discussion among present-day researchers in cutting-edge fields such as quantum physics, consciousness, healing and biology. If such a relationship does exist, it would then extend well beyond Earth and include all the planets and celestial bodies in our solar system, the constellations, galaxies, quantum fields and any other forms of creation beyond our known dimensions.

As shared by Nassim Haramein from the International Space Federation:

> One of the most fundamental errors in our human understanding of the universe is the idea that it is even possible for anything to be completely separate from anything else. Every point (and therefore every thing) in

the entire universe is connected to every-other point and thing in the universe by the SPACE that everything in the universe is defined by.

You may think of space as being empty, but science has proven that this perception is an illusion, that space is actually completely full of little tiny tiny vibrations called "vacuum fluctuations" that when all added up equal a nearly infinite amount of energy.

This field of energy that permeates the entire universe has been given a lot of names over the decades: the aether, the plenum, the zero point field, the quantum foam, the source field, the vacuum, Mana, Prana, Chi, God, call it whatever you like, the SPACE that fills everything also connects everything. Rather than thinking of matter as defining the space, realize it is space that defines matter.

There is no such thing as "separation" in the universe…"

Curiosity about the dynamics of our solar system, in particular the strange lights moving in the sky sometimes referred to as gods, spirits or angels, dates back thousands of years. Evidence of this can be found in ancient teachings of most cultures as well as in archaeological findings around the world. Observation of celestial activity contributed to the development of astronomy, mathematics, mythology, philosophy and religion. As a result of this curiosity, science expanded and new tools, techniques, technologies, knowledge and understanding emerged.

Up until a few hundred years ago, studies and research in most fields of interest were interrelated, from science to mathematics, biology, agriculture and religion, even allowing room for philosophical questions about the origins of life. In those times, curiosity about life and the universe held no boundaries. Knowledge, teachings and information were not bound by rigid rules, statutes, dogma, fixed curriculums, political or economic agendas, laws, or constraints of any kind. In this climate of openness and inquisitiveness, any and all questions were acceptable, allowing for unlimited exploration and study, thus facilitating the emergence of new knowledge and technological advancement. Curiosity was indeed a wonderful gift, and when used with wisdom, it has led to many discoveries for humankind.

Traditional astrology emerged several centuries BCE out of a long-standing curiosity about the relationships between the movement of the planets against the backdrop of the stars and constellations, and the potential impact of these relationships on earthly life. This was a time when there was great respect for nature and the cycles of life on Earth. Planetary positions and movements were studied in order to determine the best times for planting and harvesting crops, or times for celebrating seasonal changes. In Mesopotamia, relationships between the Moon and other planets were observed to determine the fate of a king and his people. This practice was likely used in far more ancient times since relationships between planetary movements and the constellations can be found in many ancient artefacts. In the late Babylonian period, the constellation on the horizon was observed for its impact on the life of an individual. The Greeks later termed this rising constellation the "watcher of the hour," the *horoscopos* or horoscope. Clearly, in those times, there was a deep sense of the natural oneness, or unity of all aspects of creation as well as mankind's integral place in a vast universe.

In time, as the Church gained more power and control in the Western world, many ancient teachings, in particular those relating to the study and practice of astrology were rejected and outright condemned. In order to maintain this control, those who ventured beyond accepted teachings were burned at the stake or tortured. Naturally, fearing torture, or worse, death, interest in non-mainstream, or unaccepted topics waned. By banning and eliminating more open or expanded perspectives, the dominance of the systems in place at the time was reinforced and sustained.

But more than that, because of this outright condemnation, the world was deprived of the wealth of invaluable insights, wisdom, and tools for self-knowledge and healing inherent in astrology as well as many ancient and indigenous teachings and practices. As a consequence, with the arrival of the industrial revolution, science, and perhaps commerce may be included here, were made to reign supreme. Anything metaphysical, beyond the three-dimensional world, or what could be measured with the tools of the day, in fact almost anything outside of accepted teachings and doctrines was deemed unacceptable, invalid, or even evil. So it is that, from that point forward, studies made in astrology and in many ancient spiritual and metaphysical subjects were deprived of the benefits they might have gained through rigorous scientific methods of research, study and analysis.

Astrology and the Horoscope

A distinction needs to be made between astrology and the familiar daily, monthly, or yearly horoscopes. Astrology is based on the calculation and evaluation of precise planetary positions relative to the backdrop of the constellations for a given date, time and geographic location. Potential traits and events are then derived from these planetary configurations, the keyword here being *potential*.

The popular horoscope, on the other hand, may not be the result of such diligent study. Truthfully, daily horoscopes never resonated with me, even when I first began to study astrology back in the late 1960s. Somehow, they didn't seem to reveal anything relevant or helpful, at least not for me. It was only many years later that I came to understand why this was so. I now know that many of these daily horoscopes are simply creations of the imagination and are not at all based on the study and analysis of celestial geometry.

In 1992, I was given the opportunity to write a bi-monthly astrology column for a local paper. In those articles, I explored the general nature of the signs of the zodiac, focusing on talents, traits, learning opportunities and potential trends. These had been fun to write because they provided me with an opportunity to explain astrology and its purpose, which was to help us gain greater self-awareness and understanding, and thus help us make better daily and long-term life choices.

Then in 1996, I was invited to write a daily horoscope for another local paper. It seems that the position had been made available when the writer of the column gave up her post. Since this was not something I had ever done before, and since I am always eager to try something new, I accepted. However, contrary to my previous article-writing experience, as it turned out the writing of daily horoscopes was a whole other matter! My task was to write a couple of lines for each sign for every day of the week, in both English and French. I would spend 50 hours a week calculating the movement of the Moon and the aspects made between the Moon and the other planets and then hypothesizing how these might relate to each Sun sign. Honestly, it was the worst job I ever had in my life and after just a couple of weeks I was ready to quit.

Luckily for me, barely a few weeks into my one-year contract the original writer of the column informed the paper that she wanted her job back. Well, let me just say that I was only too happy to let her have it! I knew then why someone would make up content for these daily horoscopes since they are, at least in my experience, incredibly difficult to write. Not being a fan of, let alone a writer of fantasy, this was definitely not the job for me. Just as you would not seek to get your science knowledge from a sci-fi movie, make sure your astrology comes from a credible source.

An astrologer friend of mine in another city later shared that she had contacted her local newspaper to see if she could write their daily horoscope. She was given the phone number of the person writing the column and told to ask if they were ready to give it up. When she did call the writer, he replied: "No way, my wife and I make it up over coffee in the morning!" Looking back now, I think it was probably a good thing that she never got that job, for I think she was more into astrology than fiction writing. On the other hand, I can understand why the original writer(s) wanted to keep it, since for them, it was fun!

Unfortunately, once astrology was banned, this allowed certain individuals to misuse and abuse the knowledge for profit, or to appear superior in some magical way. This is not to say that it was not misused in the past, only now there were no guidelines for legitimate or ethical practice. And so yes, it is understandable that some will condemn astrology for, sadly, many have been duped by such dishonest practices. But, as we all know, there can be dishonesty, lying, cheating, duplicity, corruption, abuse and misuse in any field, whether it be business, religion, education, entertainment, commerce, government, politics, medicine, science or finance. Not all advisors, practitioners, consultants, or so-called "experts" are honest or credible. Again, as with any field, a little research and due diligence can be beneficial.

Our Future Is Written in the Stars!

Well, that's not quite how it works. While it may be written on a stone, it isn't written in stone. While there may be some potential, even natural trend lines, the future is not written anywhere for, as we are now learning, we have a role to play in the creation of our future. Basically, whether we like it or not—and many will not like this at all—what we think and do today is foundational to what we will be living and experiencing tomorrow. The truth is that, in ways that may be difficult to comprehend at this time, let alone accept, we have more input in the writing of the script for our future than we realize. And so it is that many possible scenarios, or what are sometimes referred to as "timelines" lie ahead and, in fact, even lie beyond the linear timeline as we know it.

As frightening or as disturbing as this may sound, if you think about it a bit, that very fact alone gives us hope. Actually, acceptance of this fact—the fact of our essential contribution—is among the first steps in reclaiming our power and ultimately creating the world that is equal to our true potential, a world that is far greater than what we are currently experiencing, but also far greater than what we have known for thousands and thousands of years. In later chapters, we will examine the potential challenges posed by this perspective, and ways that might help us make our way through the Gateway to a new world.

This may sound strange to someone who has not studied or practiced astrology, but I was never a fan of predictions, much less prophecies. Actually, they always made me feel somewhat uncomfortable. Now you're probably scratching your head and wondering why the heck did I get into astrology in the first place? I must admit that at first, I was curious about the future. From the perspective of that "dark night of the soul" period in my youth, I was looking for a brighter future, for something that would inspire me to keep moving forward in this life. Not only did I want to know if this life would ever have true meaning and purpose, I was also looking for answers to questions that past and current teachings had not provided.

Early in my studies, I discovered that astrology was a wonderful tool for self-knowledge and self-understanding, something much more helpful than any prediction could ever be. In fact, throughout my years of practice, I rarely looked ahead in the charts, preferring to focus on current trends. If we want a brighter, better future, we need to look at where we are now and address what may stand in the way now; not in some near or far distant future. It is only in recent years that I have come to appreciate the wisdom of that unusual reticence to knowing what the future holds in store for us. The reason I was never comfortable with predictions is that I didn't want to interfere with the movement of Life that I sensed was behind All That Is, a movement that was far greater than anything I could ever perceive or even imagine, let alone understand, given my limited knowledge at the time.

The information derived from astrology and numerology was very helpful for identifying character traits, skills, aptitudes, as well as areas that might require attention for growth, learning, healing and, ultimately, for creating a better life. I used this knowledge to help facilitate the journey and to uncover the best path forward for each individual I worked with. The configurations in our personal astrology and numerology charts are simply there for our learning and reflect our unique experiences in this lifetime. Once the lessons have been learned and our innate skills have been activated, we can use them in helpful, creative, productive and fun ways. Perhaps this approach was different from that of others in the field, but it is the approach that was in alignment with my journey in this life.

There was another factor that supported my hesitation to make predictions, and that's something I again came to understand much later in life. The fact is that we have a lot more power and control over our lives than we realize. To make a specific prediction is to sow a seed. Once a seed has been sown, it is very easily nurtured in a variety of ways such as with beliefs, thoughts, expectations and emotions. One very effective way of nurturing such a seed is through the use of the energy of fear. Another is through simple, unquestioned acceptance, or belief.

For example, I had a client whose family came from Vietnam. Early in life, her mother had been told that she would die at the age of 54, and unfortunately she did. It was a seed that she had watered on a regular basis with her belief and expectation, and it eventually became her experience. Had she discarded that prediction and chosen to not nurture it, perhaps she would have lived a longer life. We'll never know. So, when clients would tell me I had correctly predicted an outcome in their life—usually a positive outcome, since I avoided gloomy predictions—I had mixed feelings. I felt good about my skill, but ambivalent about the impact I may have had. Had I interfered? I generally kept my forecasts very broad, with suggestions of how to make the best use of upcoming trends for learning, growth and healing.

The same principle also applies to ancient prophecies, in particular those dressed up in hyper-inflated drama and fear, many of which are symbolic and are not meant to be taken literally. Over time, they have become deeply engrained aspects of the programming of many cultures around the world. The world doesn't change at the end of a calendar, nor when a new year starts. Calendars, while inspired by seasonal changes, are man-made, and seasonal trends vary over time. As we will see, the world we live in is not the result of, nor is it bound by, some prophesy or predestined fate. The good news is that we have a far greater role to play in the unfolding of life in the world than we realize. Once we digest and accept this single most important fact—actually, for some, a tough pill to swallow—we can then begin to move forward and create a better world for all life on Earth. So, let us use some of our innate curiosity to help us move forward and explore what lies ahead.

> Curiosity exists in a mind free of fear, unhampered by beliefs, expectations or the need to please others, and it is fuelled by the promise of delightful discovery. (AARCT, Ch. 6, p. 86)

Perspectives

We live in an age in which we are oftentimes confounded by a deluge of conflicting, competing and contrary information. So it is very likely that if you research the subject of this book, you will find many differing opinions and perspectives. This seems to be the case with just about any subject today, as I discovered when doing a bit of research on how to grow microgreens. While I had been growing my own microgreens for over a decade, and quite successfully, I might add, I was curious to see if I could improve my technique a bit, or maybe save costs. I like to experiment and try new things; it's in the inherent nature of my 14/5 Life Path and birthday numbers, the number of R&D, as I like to call it.

For example, as I was editing this last paragraph, the timer on my stove went off. The water was boiling and ready for the chickpea and lentil macaroni I was about to test. I just love those little, seemingly insignificant synchronicities! They add a little lightness to life, something that is much appreciated these days.

The information I found on how to best grow microgreens was mind-boggling. One expert said to soak the seeds for four hours; another said to soak the seeds for twelve hours; and then another said to not soak the seeds. Plant the seeds in soil; use coconut fibre substrate; no soil needed, just use paper towels. Water them from the top; water them from the bottom. Add fertilizer; seeds don't need fertilizer. And this was only the result of my research on how to grow sunflower microgreens. Forget about the other beans and seeds! In the end, I concluded that I would continue to grow them "My Way," as the song goes. After seeing this common trend in just about every subject I researched, I guessed that if I said, "Excuse me, I burped," some expert would step in and say: "No, you farted."

I recognized that this deluge of information is natural, as each soul is working from a unique perspective during this major period of transition. The explosion of "experts" in all fields today is also a reflection of a trend that is natural to Aquarius. As Aquarius is an air sign, it is strongly intellectual and, as a fixed sign, it likes to know. That is one of its key traits: I know. Another attribute expressed through these experts is sovereignty. Aquarius is autonomous, independent and sovereign. It is only natural that it likes to have information for itself, from itself. What is important is that each person learns to go inside and gather the information that is relevant and helpful for them. Otherwise, you can be completely confused by what is out there.

So it is that the astrological perspective in this book is based on my studies and personal experience with astrology. Over forty years ago when I did my first consults, my interpretation of the astrology data was based on some fifteen years of study and learning with traditional texts and courses with the Rosicrucian Fellowship and the Faculty of Astrological Studies in the UK. So it was that, in my early years of consultation work, my interpretations of the charts were rather textbook, as were my consults. In time, I let my intuition step in, and my interpretations became more personal, allowing for a closer connection with my clients. I would prepare all the data needed before the consult including the transits, progressions and the numbers. This would take a good fifteen to twenty minutes. Yet, during all that prep time, I never got much from what I was seeing. In fact, it wasn't unusual for me to seriously doubt that I could actually be of any help during the upcoming consultation.

This would all change once I made contact with the client. Whether in person or on a video call, a connection was made whereby a picture of the person's life just "came" to me. I was then able to see things that I don't think I could have seen with traditional astrology. Sometimes it was as though I "became" the person, acting out a past or potential situation in a manner or style that would illustrate what was in the charts. Very often, the client would then laugh in agreement and surprise. In that moment, a true connection was made. Being a hands-on practical person, I did not pursue why this was so, nor did I try to get it validated by some school of study. This was how I was able to best serve my clients, and this is all that mattered.

My innate aversion to making specific predictions about the future no doubt caused some, perhaps many, of my clients to look elsewhere to have their charts read. I understand this, and I have no problem with it. We each seek out the information that we think we need now, in other words, what can help us at the current moment, given our level of understanding and consciousness. It takes a brave soul indeed to be willing to look inside, take responsibility and then step up and do what is needed.

The same applies to my perspective on the Age or Era of Aquarius. It comes from inside, from intuition, from some higher source, maybe, but it is very clear. It is from this perspective that I wrote this book. As much as I have searched for answers as to how knowledge of the planets and constellations first came to be, I have not found any clear, consistent answers. Since I am more interested in what we can do now to create a better future for our children and grandchildren, for the generations to come as well as for planet Earth, I continue to tap inside to get the information, insights and intuition needed to make this happen.

What is very clear, and what no one is likely to deny, is that change is needed—very much needed. Also, there is growing awareness of the fact that there is far more to who and what we are, as well as the fact that we belong to a much greater expanse than the 3-D or 4-D earthly experience we have been bound to for thousands of years. Therefore there is far more to be explored, to be uncovered, and to be experienced. As we become increasingly aware of the need for healing of our current situation and as we become willing to accept responsibility for the roles we have played in the past, and the role we are playing now, the transition into the new Era will be smoother and more graceful for each and every soul on Earth.

A Brief Overview of the Eras

As explained in AARCT, the Eras are periods of roughly 2,100 years based on the division of the Great Year into 12 segments. The Great Year is a cycle of approximately 26,000 years that is determined by the precession of the equinoxes—the trajectory traced by the polar axis of the Earth. Just as with any change of season on Earth, there is a transition phase of one to two hundred years between any two Eras. This transition period allows for life to adjust to the climate of the new Era, or season. This means that, as we adjust to the new season, we are playing a role—even a significant role—as we are sowing seeds for the future of life on Earth. Through our thoughts, our choices and our actions, we are making a contribution to the unfolding of the new Era. The fact is that it's not happening "to" us; rather we are actively participating in the creation of the world at this very moment.

The Eras are similar to the seasons we experience on Earth on a yearly basis. Some transitions from one season to another are quick and easy, while others may be slow and rough. Where I live in Canada, when we are transitioning between seasons, we never know how to dress. When winter comes to an end and spring begins, we can have a couple of warm days followed by the occasional cold, snowy day, or even a massive snow storm. One day we pull out sandals and shorts, the next day, we're back to boots, mitts and winter coats. Similarly, there is no precise date for the end of one Era and the start of another, nor will the shift happen overnight.

As we transition from Pisces to Aquarius, we are encountering a mixture of attributes from both climates, which may explain the seeming uncertainty and confusion, the lack of harmony and coherence experienced by humanity on the planet at this time. What can be helpful is to understand the general nature of the Eras being transitioned so we can make the most appropriate choices. For example, just as shorts and sandals may not be the best choice of attire for a cold snowy day, attempting to sustain the extensive control measures developed in our societies throughout the past

Era of Pisces will certainly not be sustainable in the new Era of Aquarius, since it is primarily aligned with sovereignty and freedom. While some systems and control measures were helpful, such as road regulations, for example, others have gotten out of hand, such as dictatorships and other forms of abuse of power. This is likely to be among the first issues addressed as we transition into the Era of Aquarius.

Another point to keep in mind is that not everyone will be thrilled about the upcoming changes. Some just love the heat of summer and absolutely hate the cold of winter, while for others, it is the exact opposite. Some love change and adventure, while others cling for dear life to the old familiar ways. So this shift will be experienced differently by each individual. Also, while snow may be in the forecast, it does not mean that you must or will prepare for a ski trip; you may want to stay at home and bake a cake. We always remain free to choose what we do, or at the very least, how we perceive what we do.

So, let's embrace the invaluable knowledge made available to us from the unbounded cosmos in which we live so we can participate in the best way possible in this major transition. Let's sort through the rubble of our crumbling, long-held structures so we can learn from the past and not bring past errors into the future. Then, let's open our hearts and begin to create a completely new experience, a completely new world for humanity, a world of equality, community, compassion, and above all, Love. This is what we can achieve in the beautiful new Era of Aquarius, but as always, this will be so if we so choose and if we are willing to do the work.

CHAPTER 3

The Demise of the God of Old

[I]n the great heart of humanity there is a deep homesickness which never can be satisfied with anything less than a clear consciousness or understanding of God... There is nothing the human soul so longs for as to know God. (*Life and Teachings of the Masters of the Far East*, Vol. 1, p. 126)

Letting Go

The reader has no doubt gathered from the first chapters, or earlier books, that my so-called spiritual journey began when I was very young, perhaps even too young, although I now see it as a blessing. This quest was fuelled by an odd feeling of not quite belonging and a deep desire to uncover the meaning of life or the truth about our existence on Earth. I recall when I was in grade school, staring outside the classroom window, and wondering what I was doing there. What was it all for? What did it mean? Why were we here? Was there more to life? Was there something beyond the physical, worldly experience? I was curious in particular about the future. What would life be like when I grew up?

The above quote from *Life and Teachings of the Masters of the Far East* clearly expresses that deep yearning. However, given my early Roman Catholic indoctrination, as I looked around a world filled with inequality, poverty, starvation, struggle, competition, divisiveness, cruelty, war and so much unfairness, it was hard to turn to "God" to fulfill that deep inner yearning. How could a loving "God the Father" allow his children to suffer so? Why would those poor unbaptized children born in Africa be judged as unworthy of the "Kingdom of Heaven" and be sent to limbo after their death? This didn't make any sense. Then, if you were lucky enough to be Catholic, you were more or less assured a place in Heaven. However, that would be the case as long as you didn't commit too many mortal sins, which would require punishment with time spent in purgatory, or even worse, eternity in hell. That "God" was one terrifying dude! Who on Earth would long to know God, let alone return "home" to Him? Not me!

Looking back now, I can appreciate one minor benefit of that frightening teaching. Besides igniting my innate curiosity about the true nature of life, it actually kept me from committing suicide, an act classified as a mortal sin by the Catholic Church. During that "dark night of the soul" period in my youth, on my way home from work I would stand at the very edge of the subway platform, just praying, taunting, wishing that someone would push me in front of an oncoming train. "Come on, push me in," I'd silently say to those standing behind me. I had no real intention of jumping in myself, since I still harboured that ever-so-tiny seed of curiosity about the meaning of life. But, if someone were to push me in, that would have been my lot, and I was okay with that. Plus, I would not have committed that dreadful punishable mortal sin and I would still be assured a place in "Heaven," or so I thought.

But no one pushed me in, nor did I jump in myself. In fact, there were moments when I had the faintest sense of a gentle hand on my right shoulder, holding me back, making sure I would not fall in, even if I was accidentally pushed in. No matter what, I was safe. I later came to know that this was Mother Mary's gentle, loving hand, and for that nurturing care I will remain forever grateful. And so it is that I am here now.

As I finished writing the first draft of these paragraphs, a birthday card I had received from a friend the day before caught my eye. It said: "Thanks for Being Born." On the shelf right above it was another card: "I'm Glad We're So Close." I just love it when the Universe speaks to me! It reminds me that we are not alone, that

CHAPTER 3 • THE DEMISE OF THE GOD OF OLD

we are loved and supported on our journeys, no matter how dark they may seem.

So it was on this foundation of fear that many of us trudged through school where we tried our best to learn what they wanted us to learn, not what we wanted to know. School was not a place to ask questions; it was a place to comply and learn the teachings of the day. Whether or not the information resonated with you was not a factor. If, for example, you wrote an essay on an 18th-century novel in which you expressed your unique perspective but your perspective was not in alignment with the teacher's, you were graded accordingly. If you were lucky, you might get a C. With math, you either solved the algebraic equation, or you didn't. End of assignment. No argument there. Unlike with other subjects, you got full marks. No wonder math was my favourite subject!

Back in grade school, you learned to follow the rules, lots of rules! First, the building was divided into two sections with the boys on one side and the girls on the other. This division applied also to the schoolyard during recess and other outdoor activities. We lined up two by two when going to and from the classroom, starting with the shortest pair up front, to the tallest at the end. I was near the back of the line.

Then there was the rigorous dress code. I recall being yanked out of the gym in front of hundreds of students by a God-serving "Mother Superior" during a celebration of sorts—probably Easter. That day, we were allowed to wear regular clothes instead of our formal tunics. I was so proud to wear the brand new sweater set my mom had bought me for that very occasion. It consisted of a beautiful white sleeveless top with pink flowers and trim and a matching long sleeve sweater.

On the way down to the gym, I made the mistake of leaving the long sleeve sweater in my locker, as it was a warm day. When the nun grabbed me, she looked at my bare arm as though it was an evil, dirty part of my body. "Go put something on," she ordered. That was humiliating for a shy ten- or eleven-year-old. I don't recall my exact age, only the humiliation. It was as humiliating as being ordered to stand in the corner for having used a French word in answer to a question in first grade. When that happened, we had just moved to the big city from a predominantly French small town up north. I was a very shy six-year-old whose mother tongue was French, just beginning to learn English as my second language. Where is the love in this world?

As we can see, the disempowerment of the individual and the seeds of divisiveness of humanity begin early in the life of the soul that incarnates on Earth. As we move forward into the new Era, there is no doubt that we will need to take a close look at how we engage with our young children. Perhaps if we listen to them rather than pontificating from a position of authority we may learn something. They are not blank slates. As we will see, these souls carry far more knowledge, wisdom and intelligence than most will credit them with.

Then, if you survived grade school, you went through puberty, became a good girl, and grew up to be as attractive as possible so you could find someone to marry. Once you had found someone, you settled down and you made babies who would then go through the same process. The cycle of life went on; you were born, you aged and then you died. But, is that all there was to life? Is that what God intended for us? Is that what a loving God was giving His children? It couldn't be! It didn't make sense. It just wasn't enough for me. There had to be more!

And so it was that in my teens, I began to delve into various subjects, from spirituality to philosophy to science—anything that might provide answers to my questions. At first, I only read books that carried the Church's stamp of approval. Just to make sure I wouldn't be breaking "God's" laws and end up in purgatory, I would always check for the *nihil obstat* on the copyright page indicating that the book was safe to read. I read mostly the lives of the saints, as I wanted to know how they did it, how they figured out what life was about, how they got to be on God's good side and made it to "Heaven." But they seemed to experience more self-denial, sadness and suffering than joy and fulfillment. These works were not inspiring at all.

In my early twenties, I enquired about joining the Cistercian monastery, wanting to follow in Thomas Merton's footsteps, my idol at the time. But that avenue was not open to women. This was most unfair, plus, as I had been taught, only priests could talk to God. So, where was the hope for women? A few years ago, a friend shared that she was taught that when it rains outside, it's the nuns mopping the floor up in Heaven. Even if I were to become a nun, I wouldn't get very far, and so I moved on in my quest. Interestingly, when I explored teachings from other cultures, whether Tibetan or Hindu, I felt safe because I had been baptized. I wouldn't burn in hell for exploring teachings that were not sanctioned by the Holy Roman Catholic Church. Wow. That's how deep the indoctrination was!

In my thirties and forties, I took a slight break from this quest, though its seeds had been deeply sowed and continued to colour my path, only now in a more subtle way. With spiritual questions temporarily placed on the back burner, I managed to live a very full life as a mother, single-parent, cook, gardener, tech writer, business owner, coach, teacher, consultant, speaker and more. Sometimes I would look back and say, "I've had six lifetimes in one!" It was a busy time, but rich and rewarding.

As it turned out, these mundane or "non-spiritual" activities were very helpful as they provided a basis from which I could better understand my clients. But more importantly, the familiarity with a wide range of human experiences opened my heart. Having "been there and done that," I knew very well what it felt like. This made it much easier to relate to others, especially those who were not "on the journey," or those who had no interest in spirituality. I would never have learned this had I spent my life in a monastery or hidden away in a cave in Tibet. Never underestimate your life experiences, as you never know what they might teach you, or what precious gems they might bless you with. In the end, first-hand experience provides the most valuable learning of all—it is the invaluable gift of knowing. And with true knowing, you can more easily come back to your heart, the place that truly matters.

Despite those busy years of middle life, the seeds of my spiritual quest did not die, nor could they be kept buried for long. So it was that when I turned fifty, as shared in *Making Peace with God*, once again I began to question the nature of God and the meaning of life. This is when *A Course in Miracles* came into my life, giving my journey a whole new direction. While it was a call I could not ignore, there was a cost to this journey: broken relationships, alienation from family, and an inability to fit in socially. No one I knew seemed interested in this quest.

However, the desire to know the truth of who and what we are was so compelling that I was ready to pay the price. Had I known what I now know, I probably would have made different choices. In fact, I'm quite certain that my interactions with others would have been different. But that was not the case. I did the best I could, given what I believed, what I knew, what I understood, but most importantly, given who and what I thought I was. Such is life in the limited human condition.

One of the most important and empowering lessons I have learned is to be able to look back at any decisions and choices made in my life and then love that soul who just did her best. There's always room for appreciation and gratitude when we look back at our life experiences. As my Guides have said so many times whenever I get caught up in the past: Let it go, let it go, let it go. Then the song by the Beatles "Let it Be" comes to mind. I take a deep breath, give myself some love, and let it all go. Loving oneself makes it much easier to let go than thinking and trying to understand and fix the past. In fact, the past can't be fixed; it can only be learned from and released. We can only fix our present perception, and choosing love is the greatest fix of all.

No doubt, everyone on the planet at this time could use a little letting go and, more importantly, a healthy dose of self-love. Look back over your life, think of a less-than-glorious moment in your past; it doesn't need to be the worst thing you have ever done, you can deal with that one later. If it makes it easier, see yourself as a child, or see the child in you. Now love yourself and give yourself a big hug. Most importantly, you must feel the love. Love is not a word; Love is an experience, and you will know it when you feel it. Try it, do it now. This is among the first steps on our journey of healing and becoming whole. We can always choose to look back and recall a situation, then feel that love and let it all go. That is true forgiveness, and forgiveness begins at home. It is a major step towards healing, as well as becoming free from boundaries and limitations of all kinds. It is among the greatest gifts we can give ourselves. It is a gift that remains always available. All we need is to claim it now; claim it now. And whether we realize this or not, when we claim it with utmost sincerity and intent, we make the greatest contribution to the healing of humanity. Forgive and let go; forgive and let go.

A Friend on the Journey

As I was approaching the start of my eighth decade on Earth, it occurred to me that my quest wasn't over yet—at least not quite. While *A Course in Miracles* and several other contemporary works had been very helpful in clearing the path to the realization of who and what we are and what we can become, I still had issues with certain concepts, God being at the top of the list—in large, bold letters. It wasn't long before I realized that my issues were more concerned with the language, or the old programming attached to the words, rather than the actual concepts. Fortunately, once recognized, this was something that could be addressed and released.

After years of intensive study of *A Course in Miracles*, given my early exposure to Catholic doctrines, there were lingering shades of the distorted, traditional "God" that needed to be cleared up. Note that my experience with the teachings of the Catholic Church is unique to me. Many people I have spoken with on this subject seem to have had a less difficult time with it; some even have had no problem at all with the teachings. Maybe some were better at daydreaming during religion class or church services. Unfortunately or fortunately—it depends on how one looks at it—that was not the case with me, as I was listening to every word being said. From what I have seen, those who are not affected by the dark indoctrination of a church or religion are more likely to conceive of a benevolent, loving God. Again, each person's journey is unique, and in that uniqueness our learning opportunities will be found.

As I continued on this journey, I noticed that whenever a teaching made use of the word "God," even a contemporary teaching that resonated with me, especially when repeated frequently, I would take a little step back—sometimes a big step. Such was the case with *A Course in Miracles* which uses the word "God" more than four thousand times, as well as the word "Father," another term with which I had issues, which is used nearly one thousand times. The masculine attribute of God—the Source of all life—did not resonate well with me. "Beyond the poor attraction of the special love relationship, and ALWAYS obscured by it, is the powerful attraction of the Father for His Son (ACIM, Ch. 15, p. 363)." His Son? What about his Daughters? And why only one son? I understood that much of what was written in this and other spiritual teachings was metaphorical or symbolic, but as one who generally takes things literally, even after years of study I still had a bit of trouble with some of this language.

While my father was a kind and sweet man, he was on the road much of the time, so he did not play a significant role in my life while I was growing up. Oh, and of course, given my innate sensitivity to—or, more accurately, my aversion to—social hierarchies and inequality, the word "kingdom," which comes up a couple of hundred times in that book, was a no-no for me. Clearly, these issues with language indicated that there were some deeply buried blockages that needed to be addressed.

If the language was a problem, why was I drawn to *A Course in Miracles* and similar works, especially channelled messages from Jeshua? As shared in *Making Peace with God*, in my youth, despite the dark side of the teachings of my religion, I had very much enjoyed the stories about Jesus, or Jeshua, as I prefer to call him.

CHAPTER 3 • THE DEMISE OF THE GOD OF OLD

> I imagined myself alongside him two thousand years ago, walking the dusty roads that took him on his healing and teaching missions, breathing the hot, dry salt air, touching the sick, comforting the desperate. I was in awe of Jesus. Unlike me, he did not seem to have any questions or any doubts. Only answers. He was kind and loving and, above all, forgiving, even in the face of the most inhumane acts. He was always in a state of peace, something I wished to attain one day too. (Ch. 2, p. 20)

I also shared a dream I had while grieving the passing of my cat Bubby.

> Deep into the night, between bouts of analysis and semi-conscious sleep, I found myself drifting and falling back in time to another place until I had a clear impression of myself as a young girl of maybe ten or eleven, hiding my identity beneath layers of clothing, hugging a rough cloak over my head. I knew I wasn't supposed to follow the others—my older brother had scolded me a number of times already, but I couldn't help myself. I was curious. I wanted to see more of the incredible man who sat and talked to the small group of men along the roadside. There were other children running and playing nearby, mostly boys, and the man seemed to like them very much, but I wasn't allowed to be there.
>
> "You must return home to help Mother prepare the bread," my brother had told me. "This gathering is for grown-ups. Go home now." But the man fascinated me. He was kind and gentle and had a smiling look in his eyes, and he seemed to love everyone. Jesus, they called him. Everyone seemed to like him. When they rose to walk on down the road to the farther reaches of town, I wanted to follow too, like my brother, but I dared not lest he find that I had disobeyed. So I stayed behind and watched until I could no longer see him. I knew he would be doing something special; I had heard that he could heal the sick. One day, I told myself, one day, I will be older and I will go with him too. (MPG, Ch. 15, p. 222)

Then one night a couple of years ago, as though a reminder of that dream, I had a vision, or perhaps it was a memory, I really don't know. I was a young girl, maybe nine or ten, walking outside with my mother. In the distance, there was a man talking to a group of people. I felt very drawn to him. Curious, I started to walk toward him. Instantly, my mother grabbed me by the arm and told me in no uncertain terms that I could not go there. That was the end of the vision. There seemed to be an ancient pattern in my history of setting out on the journey and then not being allowed to pursue it. This was a clear indication that something would need to be released. In a way, these experiences explained my attraction to the teachings of Jeshua in this life. And so it was only natural that he would be helping me on this journey. We all have Friends and Guides walking alongside us, but we will receive only as much help as we let in. So let us ask for this blessed help from our Guides, and being from love, how could they not answer our calls?

Created in the Image and Likeness of God

One of the attributes of Aquarius is that it is fundamentally experiential. Given my Moon and Ascendant in Aquarius I can certainly relate to that! One of my favourite hobbies is playing in the kitchen, trying new recipes, just having fun experimenting with techniques and ingredients. In order to truly know something, we need to see it, touch it and experience it. *A Course in Miracles* stresses the importance of this point, stating in the Use of Terms that we should seek only the experience, and not let theology delay us.

But how can you experience—or more importantly, who the hell wants to go anywhere near—a judging, punishing, condemning God who commands: Thou shalt not kill, then goes on to tell his loyal followers to stone a man to death because he cut wood on the wrong day of the week (Num. 15:32)? This God says that if you swear at your mom or dad, you should be put to death (Lev. 20:9), and of course, gay couples should also be put to death (Lev.20:13). He also says that it's okay to engage in battle if the people of a town won't hand it over to you (Deut: 20:12). You must also put someone to death for disagreeing with your laws (Deut. 17:12). Oh, and you can sell your daughter into slavery (Exod. 21:7). I guess it's okay if you need a little money. Praise the intrinsic value of the female! He also seems to really like blood sacrifices, like he was some sort of vampire (Exod. 29:12). What happened to the commandment: Thou shalt not kill? In the New Testament that Christians hold so dear, it clearly states that a woman shouldn't dress up or claim any power or authority, but should instead be submissive (Tim. 2. 9-12). And the list goes on, and on.

Even if an individual, a family or a culture has not actually read or studied these works, it is interesting to see how the attributes of this God are reflected in life on Earth. With this kind of God at the helm, is it any wonder that every page of our history includes some kind of judgment, condemnation, battle, struggle, war, divisiveness or cruelty? Or, perhaps we have it all backwards. What if the depictions of this God are actually a mirror of the human condition and are not at all representative of the true God. Is there a true God? If there was a true God, what would It be like?

This supposedly "holy" book, which so many millions hold literally against their hearts, is filled with this kind of horror, violence and nonsense. This book should be on the banned list! Fortunately for the churches or religions that base their teachings on these works, from what I have learned, people don't actually read the book. They only regurgitate what the priest or pastor, or designated representative of "God" recites at a service, or they quote popular snippets to make a point or validate their position. But then, who's to say that these sources are reliable and are actually conveying truth? If these obedient followers actually read the book themselves, would they continue to cling to it, or would they throw it out and forever wash their hands of it? Maybe I'm too lazy, or more likely, it's my impatience, but I don't have time, energy or fortitude to sift through these works and try to figure out which parts are true and might actually represent the "word of God."

Despite the distortions and misrepresentations, there is one very powerful statement found in the Bible, and it is that we were "created in the image and likeness of God" (Gen. 1:27). This statement alone may be the single most important and revealing information found in the entire work, as it holds the key to uncovering the truth of who and what we are. Yet, does anyone really know what this statement means? Do you actually believe that you were created in the image and likeness of God? And, if so, what exactly is that image and likeness? Which part of you is like God? However, what is even more challenging and may present an obstacle to the experience of God is that all are created in the image and likeness of God. Can you accept that the one person you hate the most, whether this is a family member, a former friend, or a politician, was also created in the image and likeness of God? Now that's a tall order!

That "He" was portrayed as an aggressive, violent, judging, demanding entity is understandable, given that the Bible emerged during the Aries Era (approximately 2100–0 BCE), an energy that can be competitive, aggressive and combative when expressed in lower consciousness. More importantly, Aries expresses an energy that is purely male or yang, hence the birth of the one and only, male god during that Era. Clearly, that low consciousness Aries energy is still being sustained on Earth at this time as is evidenced by ongoing wars and the exercise of power, authority and competition in all fields of activity. In contrast, the Era of Taurus (approximately 4200–2100 BCE) which held pure feminine or yin energies featured many gods and goddesses. In that Era, the peoples of Earth were more focused on mining, farming and building homes and settlements, along with the acquisition of goods and wealth, all expressions of the fixed earth sign Taurus.

While the Bible states that we were created in the image and likeness of God, it also states that we are sinners, in particular, tainted by that horrible "original sin." As such, we remain always under the watchful eye of this same all-knowing, all-seeing God from which we cannot hide. God is up there in Heaven, watching his creations down here on Earth, ready to judge and punish them for their sins. What kind of God would punish his own creations? Clearly, he is not a very loving being, and he certainly is not forgiving. If we were created in the image and likeness of God, how could we be less-than-perfect little sinners? How could an all-knowing, all-powerful God create anything that is less than perfect? If God is infinite, why does he create bodies that are finite, that suffer illness, aging, pain and unavoidable death? Does God make mistakes? None of this makes any sense.

If we believe that we were created in the image and likeness of God and if we believe in a judging, punishing God, it naturally follows that we too must be judging, punishing creatures, just like our creator. It just so happens that we are quite familiar with judgment, condemnation and punishment here on Earth. And so we stand on guard and watch for others to make errors or to disobey the laws or break the rules. Then we can accuse, judge, berate and punish them, establishing a temporary distraction and perhaps even delaying the inevitable punishment that is bound to come upon us one day. Given the deeply ingrained fear of punishment, the terror of having one's faults uncovered, this tendency to projection is understandable. What we don't want to deal with inside ourselves we project out there. It's not me, it's them. That way we can buy ourselves a little time, perhaps even feel temporarily safe.

Then, imagine the ambivalence—albeit mostly unconscious—of one who prays to this God to heal an illness or to help with a difficult life situation. What if, in answer to their prayer, they were to actually come face-to-face with this Almighty God? According to long-held beliefs and programming, since this is a judging and punishing God, but also all-knowing, this might present a problem. This all-knowing God would certainly be aware of their sins, errors and imperfection. Perhaps they would be judged to be undeserving, or even deserving of punishment. Would they still want God to answer their prayer? This realization might be enough to cause the desired outcome to be diminished somewhat or altogether abandoned. Yes, I want this in my life, but maybe not that much, at least not enough that I will have to face God, just in case I still have some sins that haven't been pardoned. Then I might have to spend some time in purgatory until my sins are absolved. Perhaps it's best to just stay with the illness or the difficult life situation.

It naturally follows that the fear of death would be a deeply ingrained aspect of our relationship with this God. Who wouldn't fear death since once we "pass over" we will face the inevitable tribunal and be judged to be either worthy or unworthy by the Almighty Lord God. There are even those who believe that to fear God is an act of reverence. So now fear is a good thing. But how can there be love when there is fear? Would a loving parent want their child to be in fear of them? Would a loving parent want their child to drop down on their knees, belittle themselves, admit to their faults and beg for forgiveness all the while holding up an arm just over their forehead in anticipation of being struck? Is that what a loving father or mother does?

Given the irrationality of our teachings and belief systems, it's starting to look more like this "God" was created in the image and likeness of man, or perhaps created in the image of some less-than-divine entity, perhaps even a being from another galaxy or dimension. To be in fear, to judge, punish, rule, enslave, compete, segregate, divide, conquer, demean, control, murder, steal, berate, torture and engage in warfare, are human traits, as evidenced in the systems we have built and implemented on Earth over several millennia. Sadly, these systems are still very much in place at this time. And they certainly do not convey the kind, unifying, understanding, creative, generous, infinitely abundant, forgiving and compassionate attributes one would expect of a loving Creator/Source, Mother/Father/God. As such, it seems that we have absolutely no idea of what the true God is really like.

It is no wonder that so many people are turning away from traditional religions as we enter the Age of Aquarius, an energy that demands rationality and logic, but above all, firsthand, tangible experience. Throughout the Age of Pisces, an energy that supported blind faith, as well as all manner of systems and hierarchical structures, it was easy to build and maintain systems that did not quite reflect the Truth. Furthermore, the systems built during that Era were designed to benefit a very few, namely those in power. Looking back, we can see how the systems currently in place remain designed so the few can have control over the masses. This clearly will not be sustainable in Aquarius, an Age of sovereignty, individuality, independence and freedom.

The Age of Aries carried the energies of power and authority. During that Era, the masses were trained, under the threat of torture and death, to hand over their power to the rulers in place at the time. It is understandable that the idea of the one, all-powerful God emerged in that Era, since Aries is focused on the one in power, or the one with the most authority. As this authoritative energy was carried into the Era of Pisces, it was easy for those in power to build and maintain complex systems and structures since the masses had already been trained to comply under the threat of death.

In this new Era of Aquarius, blind faith, meaningless teachings, corrupt structures of governance, debilitating, untruthful and disempowering systems of education will fall by the wayside. But, what will replace these long-held systems? What will happen to our long-standing beliefs? What will we do with the ancient structures on which our beliefs are founded? How will we answer important questions about our origins, about who and what we truly are? There is no denying that we are here, but where does life come from? Is it all an accident? Will it all one day implode and disappear? The energy of Aquarius has not been experienced on Earth in 26,000 years, so we have no idea of how humanity fared as life transitioned into this energy in the past. We are headed into the unknown.

Clearly I was in need of some help, especially if I was going to heal that rift in my relationship with God. I wanted to know God, but it had to be a new God. And so, the journey continued.

CHAPTER 4

Reknowing God

When teaching is no longer necessary, you will merely KNOW God. (ACIM, Ch. 4, p. 71)

Where to Begin

It was early morning, my usual writing time. As I lay on my back doing some gentle leg and arm movements to release the tension from my neck and shoulders before heading to the computer, I tried to formulate a clear picture of how to organize this next chapter. I was struggling with how to write about experiences that seemed so multilayered or unusual that they were difficult to describe in words. When I tried to explain one vision to a couple of friends, words had failed. I had to show what I had seen with my arms waving up and down. The problem with words, I realized, is that they often have old meanings attached to them, and these experiences simply didn't fit anything old. Plus, it was as though I had to release everything I thought I knew, basically forget about everything I had learned and studied throughout my life so that I could be ready to experience something new and then figure out how to share it in my writing.

Most of the time, I like to have music playing in the background at home, my favourites being the jazz standards and smooth jazz. But when I write, I switch to one of the classical stations because lyrics interfere with my writing process. Since this was writing time, the television was already set to Stingray Classic Masters. Curious to know what was playing, I glanced up at the television screen. My attention was immediately drawn to the upcoming piece. No way, I thought, as I chuckled and shook my head. But by then, I was totally accustomed to coincidences or, as some like to call them, synchronicities.

The piece that was just about to start was Rachmaninoff's Piano Concerto No. 2. Knowing full well what to expect, I got up, grabbed a tissue and decided to remain there until the end. Within minutes, the tears were flowing. Music, I sighed deeply. During those difficult years of my youth, books had been my friends while music had been my medicine. I suppose I should not have been surprised when, over fifty years later, music actually became like a very real, potent medicine. But more on that later.

Wiping away the last of my tears after being carried away by that glorious third movement, I got up, returned to the computer and began sorting through my notes on the subject at hand: reknowing God. "We can do this," my Guides reassured me. "Yes," I replied, as I took a full, deep breath. "Indeed we can."

The Gods of Ancient Times

There are pros and cons to exploring ancient history and even current world events. On the one hand, the information gleaned may stir up fear, anger, resentment, hatred, frustration, depression, and a sense of powerlessness. These reactions are typically followed by a desire for vengeance or retribution disguised as a call for justice. "Someone must pay for those atrocities! They must be held accountable! Arrest them! They must be put to death!" we cry out in indignation. Given the nature of the systems and structures in place along with the current level of consciousness of the world in which we live, these responses would normally be considered entirely justifiable and even acceptable.

On the other hand, the same information could inspire a desire to let go of the old so we might, once and for all, elevate our consciousness to new heights. We could then reach up and claim an entirely new experience of Being for all life on Earth. By engaging the incredible power of forgiveness, by releasing the past as well as the present, we would then be free to focus on initiating true change. A solid foundation for healing, growth, abundance, peace, and wholeness for all life on Earth would then be established. This high level of change can only be brought about through heart-centred awareness, compassion, inclusiveness, equality, acceptance, respect and understanding. This is what more and more souls are now calling for. With open hearts, many are ready for radical—"from the roots"—change. Together we stand; yes, together we can do this!

While my research into our ancient history had strengthened my desire for a better life on Earth, it had also stirred up some deep-seated anger and resentment. There seemed to be a need for a bit of healing if I was to move on and have a new experience of God, or whoever, or whatever this Source of Life was. There were still shades of that frightening, selective, judging, punishing, dominating male God wearing a long white robe looking down on us mere mortals that needed to be released.

What helped me let go of some of my misgivings about traditional religious teachings were the narratives that have recently emerged about extraterrestrial influences on Earth. This topic has grown rapidly in popularity over the past few decades following the discoveries of possible extraterrestrial contact and likely evidence of UFO and UAP sightings. The works of Zecharia Sitchin and Michael Tellinger, among many, propose a history that is completely different from what is taught in traditional religions, cultures and educational systems. While mainstream historians, scientists, theologians and archaeologists generally criticise and dismiss these works as flawed, unproven or outright false, given that they present a picture of our history that is remarkably mirrored in today's world, they may be worth considering.

I have long accepted that, if the source of life is infinite, life must also exist in other galaxies, and very likely in dimensions and timelines that would be nearly impossible to comprehend by those bound by the 3-D linear perspective. Actually, is it not rather arrogant to believe that humans are the most evolved life forms on Earth, let alone the only sentient beings in the entire universe?

In all likelihood there are beings on other planets and in other dimensions that are less advanced than humans, as well as beings that are far more advanced. The idea of visitations by beings from places beyond Earth does not seem far-fetched at all. Actually, when looking at the larger picture, it seems very plausible.

Since a *Star Wars* piece by John Williams is playing while I am working on this paragraph, it might be interesting for the reader to know that as Aquarius is very much in tune with science, it is not surprising that science fiction books and movies have exploded in the last few decades. Given what we are learning about who and what we are, is it any wonder that we have a fascination for stories of heroes with superpowers, or extra-terrestrials who travel the galaxies where "no man/woman has gone before"?

The new depictions of our history based on recent archaeological findings suggest that beings from other planets, galaxies, solar systems or even other dimensions visited Earth in pre-biblical times, perhaps even up to, and very likely more than 200,000 years ago. In cultures around the world, there are accounts of angel-like or non-human, highly-advanced beings coming down from the "heavens" as well as depictions of vehicles or "chariots" transporting these beings to and from Earth. The term "Heaven" was no doubt coined in reference to dimensions or levels of reality that were, at the time, inconceivable and unattainable. This interaction with advanced, extraterrestrial beings may be how the seeds of curiosity about planets and galaxies were originally sown in ancient Greece, Mesopotamia and Egypt. Without the help of highly developed beings, how could a guy riding a camel through the desert ever conceive of a relationship between a constellation or a planetary configuration and events on Earth?

The new light being shed on our ancient history suggests that these visitations were not made by an almighty, infinite, all powerful, loving God or by divine or equally powerful and loving heavenly angels. Instead, they suggest that Earth was visited by beings that possessed highly advanced skills and technologies. Clearly, these abilities and this knowledge was unknown by humans on

Earth at the time. It is therefore understandable that the primitive hunter-gatherer human would perceive these beings as "gods" since they demonstrated capabilities that were far beyond what they could comprehend or even imagine.

While these beings may have appeared to be far more advanced than the humans inhabiting the planet at the time of their visitations, it appears that they were still not fully "enlightened" or of the highest possible level of consciousness or expression. They could be competitive, divisive, greedy, jealous and possessive, and were not above violence, aggression, murder and war. "I don't like these humans; they're getting out of hand. They must be destroyed," one brother says. The more compassionate brother rushes over to his human friends and says, "Go build an ark, a flood is coming." This story depicts behaviour that was clearly more super-human-like than divine, or God-like.

This perspective explains the portrayal of a biased god who would favour one group of people over another. This could not be the true God. A truly loving, all-encompassing Creator would not favour one of Her/His/Its creations over another; how could that be, since, supposedly, She/He/It created them all? Why does the "angel" save a village from an oncoming flood? Is it because he has a vested interest in keeping its inhabitants alive as he needs them to be his servants or slaves? A true angel would never demean a child of God in that way. Besides, a true angel would know that the origin of all life is pure angel-like, and that one village is not of higher value than another.

The idea of God thousands of years ago was limited to the level of conception, understanding and acceptance of which humans were capable at the time. Bound by a 3-D, survivalist, birth-life-death frame of reference, humans could not conceive of an integrated, multidimensional, all-inclusive, infinite, quantum, Creator Source. Instead, they did their best given what they perceived, knew and understood at the time, and so they made up a superior man-god who resided in some lofty Heaven up in the sky. This man-god was used to build and maintain the structures of society and thus keep the lowly human in line.

I must admit that, at first, I was more than a little miffed by the stories of genetic engineering of human DNA by these extraterrestrial beings for the purpose of enslaving humans as described by Michael Tellinger in *Slave Species of the Gods*. But, I couldn't help but acknowledge that these tales about superior beings with god-like attributes actually resembled many of the stories found in our traditional religions and mythologies. Plus, certain attributes of these powerful ancient beings, or gods, are quite evident in our present-day social, educational, economic, political, religious and world structures. In every corner of the world, one can find greed, competition, divisiveness, war, hierarchies, punishment, all of which are under the control of those in power at the cost of the disempowered, enslaved and impoverished. There's nothing new here.

These tales also explained the deeply-rooted human propensity for idolatry, whether it be for some god or a famous athlete, actor, politician, scientist, writer, business person, spiritual teacher, expert or "influencer," as some are now called. This hierarchical perspective may, in part, be a reflection of the very ancient practices of favouritism, control and enslavement by superior beings during their visits on Earth. Humans don't realize that even if they drive their own car and have a job that pays the bills, many are still slaves. Most people are working for some company, making the owners rich, while they are not doing what is in their heart. Some may have a list of things they would like to do once they retire, should they live that long. They do not require or expect to do what they truly desire, thereby diminishing their worth and limiting their expression as Divine creations of Source.

What we know of as the middle class appears then to be nothing more than glorified enslavement. This is an ancient, worn-out way of life that will not be sustained in the Era of Aquarius. This new Age will be fuelled by a desire for freedom, equality, a sense of community and inclusiveness, creative self-expression, sovereignty, respect for our home planet, but above all, a sense of self-worth—a fixed attribute of Aquarius. All of these characteristics are the complete opposite of what has been experienced on Earth for thousands of years, where humanity has known fear, divisiveness, competition, hierarchies, control measures and especially, deprecation or diminishing of self. In contrast, throughout the Era of Pisces—a mutable sign—worth was determined by standards, rules and regulations. This kind of structure will not be sustained in Aquarius.

So it appears that the gods of ancient times were simply more advanced beings. They lived beyond the boundaries of the 3-D, human experience, and were gifted with skills and abilities clearly unknown to the human on Earth at the time. This new perspective on angels and gods totally made sense. It also removed the dark, less-than-divine traits of the traditional God and higher beings. The true God was thus disentangled from our familiar stories, teachings, belief systems and religions. Still, even those higher, more advanced or evolved beings, regardless of their behaviour, regardless of which galaxy or dimension they came from, originated from somewhere. Where was *their* God? Who was their Creator? Was it the same as our Creator?

In most cultures around the world, there is great reverence for ancient teachings, and so it is easy to understand why there is much excitement as prehistoric artefacts are unearthed and translated. Will these ancient teachings serve us now? How have they served us in the past? Here we are, with a very long—and tired—history of all sorts of myths, traditions, stories and teachings. Where have these teachings brought us? Can they take us further ahead on our journey today? Can they take us beyond the known? Do we have what we need to shift to a completely new—a completely different—experience for humanity? Does anyone know who and what we truly are? Are we truly the offspring of a Divine Creator? More importantly, while many of these revised stories of our ancient history made sense, they still did not answer my question: Who or what is the true God?

> God does not understand words, for they were made by separated minds to keep them in the illusion of separation.

Words can be helpful, particularly for the beginner, in helping concentration and facilitating the exclusion or at least the control, of extraneous thoughts. Let us not forget, however, that words are but symbols of symbols. They are thus twice removed from reality. (ACIM, Manual for Teachers, p. 54)

Pure Life

As we do with everything, we naturally label and assign attributes to the Source, Creator, Spirit, All-That-Is or God based on culture, education, tradition as well as the current level of understanding and beliefs. However, most likely the Source of All Life possesses attributes that are far beyond the comprehension of someone bound by the 3-D physical dimension, basically, all humans on the planet at this time, and perhaps even beings in other galaxies or dimensions. The idea of a man-God may, for a time, have provided reassurance or comfort in the face of the great unknown or an infinite nothingness. For some, it can be helpful to personify God as it may make it easier to trust and engage in communication with It/Him/Her. Such a God would appear more approachable. It may also make it easier to see God in others. On the other hand, the idea of a God that is not human-like can be frightening because it puts us face-to-face with a force or potential power that is completely unknown, something that lies beyond our control.

While conceiving of a "friendly" God may be helpful, it is important to pay attention to the qualities or attributes assigned to this personified God, since these will determine and very likely establish boundaries to an experience of this God. For example, if you believe that this God will require that you make amends for your grave errors, or pay for your sins, very likely you will carry a certain amount of fear of this God. This fear may lead to resistance or delay in meeting this God. Besides, who on Earth has not made mistakes—which is really what a "sin" is, since, having known better, different choices would no doubt have been made. But, how much more "better" knowing is needed in order for us to make better choices?

Assigning as few traits as possible may be helpful in allowing for a greater openness to the unknown, for certainly, from our current perspective this God is unknown. For some, it may be easier to simply trust that there is something good, whole, loving, and supportive out there, beyond the known, without the potential limitations of specific attributes. Regardless of our beliefs, there is no denying that there is a powerful force behind all of creation, a force that is nurturing, supporting and sustaining all life on Earth and beyond.

In AARCT, I shared an exercise whereby you can test the meaning of words by how they make you feel.

> Sit quietly in a comfortable chair. Close your eyes and take a couple of deep breaths. Bring up a word, for example, God or Father, and let the feeling in. Not everyone was taught that God was a loving Being. Not all women will be comfortable with the term Father. See if it brings up memories, discomfort, anger, resentment or lack of trust. Not everyone had a loving relationship with their father, and so to use Father as a term for God may not necessarily inspire a desire to get reacquainted.
>
> The word you use to represent God should be free of fear or negative emotions of any kind. It should encourage closeness, trust, comfort, safety. If not, try another word such as Creator, Source, Source Energy, Supreme Being, Divine Source, Originator, Father/Mother, Allness, One Mind. If none of these work, make up your own word. Oneness has also been used in many ancient teachings, as it reflects the unity, wholeness and harmony of creation. You should experience a pull, a desire to join with this Creator/Source/God, for its essential nature is Love, and love, as we know, feels good. (AARCT, Ch. 6, p. 94)

I must admit that while the many wonderful, inspiring spiritual teachings I had encountered on this lifelong journey had gifted me with a deep understanding of the meaning of life, there was still something missing. Somehow, as much as I had worked on releasing the negative programming I had acquired through lifetimes of spiritual and religious indoctrination, the idea of a God, the Creator of all, still held me back a bit. Whenever I meditated and connected with God, or when I did my walking meditations, breathing in God and breathing out love, although it felt wonderful, and I did have a couple of incredible moments of closeness to God, those moments would inevitably fade. Then God returned to just being an idea or a word. While I had accepted the concept of a Source of All, or a God, I needed to experience more of It. After all, there must be a Creator, a God, right? But, was it really possible to know God? Can we really feel the Love of God? Is God even loving, or is that just wishful thinking on the part of us humans desperate to know true Love?

All of this pondering about who or what God is, who and what we are, left me facing a void. What if there is no God? What if all of creation is just one big huge accident of nature—a random, unintentional burp of quantum energy? I was given plenty of time to ponder these questions during an illness I experienced in the summer of 2022. As many know, there's nothing like an enforced timeout where all you can do is lie down in bed and wait for the body to heal. I had fallen ill with what started out as severe muscle pain, to the point where I couldn't lie down, and then the worst sore throat I'd ever had in my life. I couldn't eat, couldn't even swallow my own saliva. Around midnight on the sixth day of the illness, I passed out and crashed my skull on the kitchen floor—note that the ceramic kitchen floor isn't the best place to land when you pass out! After an ambulance ride to the hospital, getting my head stitched, and being put through dozens of tests and scans, it was concluded that I had a rare type of strep throat. Then I needed time to recover. So, plenty of opportunity to ponder.

Be careful of what you ask for! What I had been asking for was to know my full, True Self, my Higher Self, or my Christ Self. I was tired of the quest. I wanted answers. I wanted to know who and what we are. It then occurred to me that perhaps that was why I had fallen ill. I was now facing a crossroads where I could really know my Higher Self, since in my condition, I had no choice but to reach up and out and claim it. Oddly enough, the contrast between being in physical pain, exhaustion and powerlessness and the knowing that we are more—that I am more—was actually incredibly exhilarating. I could see it; I could grasp it; there was more.

I had been at death's door a few years earlier when my body had experienced a severe reaction to an antibiotic, but this was different. I knew I was not going to leave anytime soon, even though I was well aware of the fact that it is so peaceful on the other side—more peaceful than anything I had ever known in this lifetime. I had made the choice to remain here on Earth so I could complete the journey, and I made this choice once again. My goal wasn't to raise my consciousness, ascend, float up to Heaven and forever leave planet Earth behind. My goal was to claim my full consciousness and be here on Earth and continue to serve, in the best way I could. In truth, I wanted to walk on Earth as Jeshua had at the start of the Era of Pisces, only now with the learning needed as we transition into the Era of Aquarius.

What came to me during that quiet time of rest and healing was that I needed to let go of my fears about writing or speaking out. "Speak your truth!" my Guides said. Then my friend Mike sent me an email in which he shared a vision he'd had of the light blue light in my throat area. I pulled out one of my books that described the chakra system and read about the throat chakra. There it was: my extreme sore throat was reflecting my fear of expressing myself, fear of being judged and condemned, a very ancient long-standing fear I had carried into this lifetime. Well, that made sense! My throat was burning in pain, I could barely swallow my own saliva, so clearly, my throat chakra, associated with communication and expression, was crying out. I needed to release the fear and simply speak my truth. Very well, I concluded. I'll crawl out of my cave, write this book and share my journey to the best of my abilities.

Still, I had questions about the body. It seemed like such a harsh school for learning. My Guides provided the following insights:

"The body is a wonderful vehicle. If you release your ancient misgivings about the body, you will have a wonderful experience."

Really? How can that be; everything hurts, the body is not in good condition right now. This is not a wonderful experience.

"This is a perfect opportunity to practise patience and in particular, self-care and self-love."

Okay, I get it; patience is by far not my strong suit. But, I was taking good care of the body; that much I was capable of. I understood that it was the garment I wore while in this world, here on Earth. I needed to love and honour it as it was the vehicle that allowed me to interact with others in this dimension. Most importantly, it allowed me to continue with my own learning. But how can we experience more while in the body? We are bogged down by so much history. There is so much unlearning needed. How long will this take? I still had many questions, and clearly, my impatience was getting the best of me.

"Yes you are learning that you can be more, that you *are* more, but you have long forgotten this. It is not something that is easy to accept and experience from your current limited frame of reference. Don't look at it as a linear, historical experience based on a timeline. There is an aspect of multi-dimensionality that you are not experiencing yet, at least not fully. This multi-dimensionality is alive right here, right now. But you are making tremendous headway. You should love yourself for your efforts as we love you."

So, I guess all this digging into the past wasn't going to provide me with the answers I was looking for.

"Yes, that is why we do not dwell on the history of archaeology and anthropology, etc. You won't find the answers in the past. It is time for a new experience now, and this new experience is not dependent on or even tied to the past."

Okay, that was reassuring. Then I was advised to let go of the past; let it all go. And so I did. I let it all go, all the history, and the stories, all the teachings—well, at least as much as I was aware of at the time. Then I began to see more clearly. No history, no past, no stories. After another week of recovery, finally, I saw it. I was inspired to replace the word "God" with a word that would resonate more easily with me, the simplest, yet most revealing word: Life. And I was shown that it should be capitalized. Then all of a sudden, as I lay there connecting with this Source/God but now calling it Life, I started to see sparkles of gold and violet and other coloured energies flowing into my body. I saw the magnificent healing power flowing through the cells of the body; I felt how this body is part of the loving expression of the flow of Life. And as I loved my body and marvelled at the flow of Life, I came to know this Source as Pure Life.

Then I saw that at the core of my being, I Am; I Am Pure Life. I saw how this Pure Life flowed into every cell of the body and brought about its healing, albeit slowly, yet there it was. I am more than this body, I Am Pure Life flowing, expressing, and being ever in motion. As I lay there, soaking in that most exquisite energy, I felt—*I knew*—God, the infinite Pure Life that is the Source of All That Is. It wasn't just a word; it was a knowing through the experience of feeling, seeing, closeness, by the acknowledgement of Its very existence, Its presence in All That Is.

Regardless of age, gender, race or cultural affiliation, we colour and dress-up that flowing life energy we call the body, effectively forgetting what we truly are at our core—Pure Life, flowing, living, expressing Itself. We give it definitions based on our experiences in the body, and then we forget what we truly are. The Source of what I am, the Source of who we are, is Pure Life in expression, untainted by experiences, long-held beliefs or traumas. We simply are Pure Life.

The Great Balance

While what I had learned and experienced was for me a giant leap, questions still remained regarding the nature of creation and this Pure Life Source. Also, there was the matter of how could we approach it; how do we communicate with it. It still sounded a bit vague, maybe even a bit cold. It wasn't human-like, you couldn't negotiate with it or pray to it or ask it to fix things for you in the same way you could with a Mother/Father/God figure. Also, it was easy to point the finger at the personified God: He made me do it; I'm just following His laws; He withheld this from me; He will punish me for my sins. But, this was not as easy to do with a vague undefined Pure Life Source concept. We were taught that if we were good, God had a special place for us in Heaven. How could a vague Life Force, no matter how pure, compete with that?

Then I was shown that creation is a process whereby energy, thought, desire and many other layers of expression flow together harmoniously in a balanced way. When out of balance, the movement of creation becomes distorted or corrupt, and must then be recycled so that it can correct and rebalance itself. There must be an underlying principle of balance and harmony otherwise creation would self-destruct. The Creator/God or Life principle could not have survived billions of years in a state of imbalance, inner struggle, competition, greed, fear, battle and turmoil.

Balance occurs because the core creative Life Force remains always centred. Since the Creator is the Creator of All That Is, there can be no external stimulus that could cause it to become distracted, fearful, or imbalanced in any way. This means that it does not know or experience fear, lack, war, greed, shame, guilt or judgment, nor does it need to defend or protect itself from something outside of itself since there is nothing outside of itself. Nor can it take sides, or favour one aspect of its creations over another, as it would be expressing imbalance at its core.

In a state of internal division, or imbalance, it would essentially run the risk of meeting its own demise. Furthermore, how could it remain itself if it destroyed half or even just one small portion of itself? What would it then become? To be centred is to be neutral, not preferring one over another, but simply allowing all aspects to flow in the most appropriate and harmonious way possible. Pure Life, God, Source creates, flows and expresses. It remains always whole, perfect and infinite. The Creator must therefore be centred, neutral, peaceful, inclusive, accepting and loving of all of its creations. Such is the nature of Creation.

The original infinite Creator Energy must include everything that is in Creation since it is the Creator of All. Life flows, and sometimes stumbles, but it keeps on flowing. There is no stopping it because it is its nature to simply flow and express itself. It should not be stopped, because when you stop Life from flowing, you interfere with that which is natural. Forget about the stumbles, the mistakes or the errors, as they are simply a natural part of the expression of Life. Let Life flow, just like the river will flow over and around rocks and debris. Regardless of what is on its path, Life will find a way to keep flowing. Such is the nature of Pure Life.

Next, I was shown a different way of seeing the Catholic "Holy Trinity" of God the Father, his special, favourite Son, and that vague Holy Ghost. These forces were now presented as Life, Love and Light. Interestingly, from the perspective of numerology, all 3 words begin with the letter L which has a value of the number 3. The new trinity of Life, Love and Light very eloquently replaced the Father, Son and Holy Spirit of my early education, which are traditionally perceived as male, and are also inaccessible in that they are superior to mere mortals. They are not you; they are apart from you. And so you cannot easily integrate those energies within yourself. On the other hand, Life, Love and Light are very easy to call into one's experience. And naturally, as they are aspects of Pure Life, they express and flow in harmony and in balance throughout all of creation.

Releasing the Past

In AARCT I shared how, the year of my 65th birthday, to my utter surprise, I was guided to get a piano and sign up for lessons. Given that music had played an important role throughout my life, I didn't have to be nudged more than once. It was with great joy that I bought a keyboard and signed up for some jazz and blues and eventually beginner classical courses. As I was tied up with writing and consults, and then health issues, I didn't have much time for lessons and practice, but I did manage to learn a few songs. What was strange was how some of these songs moved me to tears—and

I'm not the crying type. I had been a fan of various styles of music since childhood, however, other than a tear now and then, music never really made me cry.

In one of the beginner courses I was introduced to "You Raise Me Up" composed by the Norwegian-Irish duo Secret Garden, a song I was not familiar with at the time. I looked it up and found the version performed by Josh Groban. Well, it actually took me a couple of days before I could listen to it without crying my eyes out. The song reached deeply, showing how we are not alone, how loving help is made available to us at all times. Whether or not this was the original meaning intended for the lyrics, I felt how, with the help of our Guides, we are called to rise above our challenges, our limitations, and all of our boundaries, so we can rise up to more than we can be.

The next song that struck me deeply was "If I Ruled the World" written by Cyril Ornadel and Leslie Bricusse, and so beautifully performed by Tony Bennett. This song was not in my piano course. Instead, it appeared on the Jazz Standards playlist, my daily background music when I am not writing. To this day, it still brings tears to my eyes. This song resonated with my deep desire for the healing of humanity, for inclusiveness, compassion, and a sense of community where the needs of all are met, a beautiful world where everyone is free, where everyone is heard, where heads are held up high. It was for me the song that heralded the beginning of the beautiful new Age of Aquarius.

These experiences were strange because as much as I loved music, it never really made me cry, at least not like this. What was going on? Then, in the fall of 2022, I attended a live concert where an original composition from my brother was premiered. It was a beautiful piece, composed in memory of the victims of the massacre in Bucha, Ukraine ("Hymne," opus 51, for string orchestra, by Michel R. Edward). Well, not surprisingly, as much as I tried not to make a fool of myself in public, it brought tears to my eyes. For those familiar with astrology, you may be interested to know that the composer of that piece was born in February of 1962, on a day when there were six planets in Aquarius. This particular celestial configuration generated a very strong pulse of equality, compassion, inclusiveness and community on Earth, perhaps sowing one of the biggest seeds in the current shift in consciousness.

Fortunately, we were sitting in a booth, away from the crowd, because the second piece on the program was Rachmaninoff's Piano Concerto No. 2. Here I could only bury my face in my jacket. Fortunately it was cold in the room, I scrunched down into the seat, lifted my jacket collar along the sides of my face and I just cried. I cried so hard, I was shaking until I felt as though I would pass out. There was no way I could control what I was feeling. The more I watched the musicians in the orchestra playing together, not competing, just creating this beautiful, exquisite music, the more I cried. This was humanity being together, expressing feelings and creating great beauty and harmony together. There was not one better than the other; together they played. This was not the first time that this piece had caused me to fall apart. Clearly, there was something in Rocky's—as I like to call him—music that resonated deeply with me, but I still did not know what it was.

A couple of months later, I attended another event where I was once again surprised by my tears. Halfway through the first part of the concert, Jules Massenet's "Meditation" from Thaïs was performed. While it was a piece I was familiar with, actually it is among my favourites, it had never made me cry. This time, tears started to flow. Then, when the operatic trio Lyrico joined in for the last piece of the first half of the programme, I couldn't hold back the tears. Who would not be moved by "Con te partiro" ("Time To Say Goodbye"), an exquisitely beautiful piece made popular by Andrea Bocelli? I wasn't expecting to be hearing these pieces, let alone to be shedding tears, since this was supposed to be a Christmas concert.

I was relieved to see that the second half of the program consisted of popular Christmas songs, pieces that would not likely move me to tears, or so I thought. However, midway through that part of the programme they sang the "Ave Maria." Well, again, I just broke down. Then I felt so confused. What was happening to me? I had listened to music all my life, and of course, shed a few tears on occasion, but this was total breakdown.

Then I sensed the presence of one of my Friends, one of my Guides, Mother Mary. She then lovingly assured me that there was nothing wrong with me, that it was my profound compassion and empathy that were being released and that I was opening up, and that was good. It was time to begin to live it. Then I understood how easy it was to ignore feelings, even when deeply entrenched in spiritual teachings. These teachings can be turned into just words or theories or beliefs. Without feeling, a teaching is incomplete. I took a deep breath, straightened myself out of my seat and wiped away the tears. Fortunately, the remaining songs on the program were basic popular Christmas tunes. I had shed enough tears for one concert.

A couple of months later, while preparing breakfast and getting ready to write, I asked the question: How can I serve? This is more like a daily morning affirmation or prayer, than a question. It's a statement I make to align myself with Source, in order to get the best possible start to the day. This time, there was an answer: "You can best serve by being your full Self." Of course, I smiled.

What I was not expecting was another dose of musical medicine. At 10 a.m. that morning, Mozart's Requiem began to play on the Classical station. When it reached the Agnus Dei, I decided to take a break from the computer and head for the living room, letting myself sway with the music. It wasn't long before the tears began to flow, or rather, pour. I took my usual spot on the floor with the intent of doing a few stretches, but ended up lying still, in tears. At one point the crying was uncontrollable; I was shaking from head to foot. Then I felt as though I had been ripped out of my body and thrown back in time a few hundred years. There I stood, at the bottom of a long, barren hill. There was a castle far up at the top of the hill. The Aquarius in me had never liked stories about castles and royalty, or hierarchies of any kind. As I listened to the music, I cried, and I cried and I cried.

While in tears, I was guided to let go of all the resentment and hatred for those who had misused and abused the servants of that time, and of any time. I was crying so hard I thought to myself, I hope the phone doesn't ring. And of course, the phone rang in that very instant. It was my friend Veronica who lives down the hall. As I was not able to hold back my crying, I accepted her offer to come up and visit. When she came through the door, she hugged me and held me. I was still shaking from head to foot. It was such a big release, like nothing I had ever felt before.

From what I have learned, I am not the only one letting the tears flow when listening to music. Actually, I was relieved to read in a YouTube comment section just how many people are moved to tears with certain pieces of music. As it turns out, shedding those tears can be very helpful in healing and releasing deep, ancient wounds. When I was young, I was told not to cry. As the obedient child I was, I kept it all inside. Now, I just let it out, well, at home, not necessarily in public. When I grew curious about my increasingly soft heart and my refusal to obey the command to not cry, I was told once again from guidance that our hearts are opening up and crying allows us to connect with the heart-centred part of our being, the part of us that we must now fully integrate into our experience.

Would it surprise the reader to know that the morning I was working on this section the piece playing on the Classical station was Mozart's Requiem? The great beauty of life moving in synchronicity is an overwhelming experience.

The New God

While I had shared my love of music in my previous books, these strange experiences are not something I had ever considered, or imagined—or even heard of. Needless to say, they had a major impact on me, probably greater than anything else in my life. Music, from what I discovered, is so much more than just sound, and most people I know have a song or two that has touched them deeply. Music is a form of expression of the soul, a way to share feelings, emotions, even thoughts that may not otherwise be understood or shared.

After doing a bit of research, I learned that my reaction to Rachmaninoff's Piano Concerto No. 2 was due to my alignment with his struggle. His desire to move forward had been held back by his deep fear of failure and complete loss of self-confidence after a poor performance of his First Symphony. After listening to the piece many times, after having cried to the point where I thought I was going to pass out, I finally was able to listen without falling apart. Sure there were tears—okay, lots of tears—it's such a beautiful piece, as are all of his four piano concertos, but I was able to hold it together—well, mostly. I realized that the struggle expressed in his music mirrored my own inner struggle, my desire for more and my doubt about my worthiness for reaching that more, that Higher Self I so desired to know. Once I realized this, I began to feel tremendous relief and joy, but most of all I felt a renewed empowerment. This is something I could achieve. This is something we can all achieve, each and every one of us, because this is who and what we truly are—expressions of Pure Life, children of God. At our core, we can only be Divine Beings for that is what Pure Life creates.

Through the healing power of music, somehow, all the old attributes assigned to God, my Catholic upbringing, even a lot of New Age spiritual jargon, were removed. It was all gone. Finally I was liberated from the ancient, false, distorted, fearful, misleading, distracting attachments to that word. I had gathered several pages of notes, comprised of words, to start working on this chapter. But in the end, there are no words to describe God. Besides, God is not a word. And humans just love to assign words to everything! If you are not feeling anything when you use the word God in your prayers or in your calls for help, you probably don't really know God, and so most likely you are just repeating meaningless empty words. God is a feeling; God is Pure Life in expression. It is just a word we use to describe something that is wordless, something that is impossible to describe in words. It is only in the experience that you will know God. Seek only the experience.

I was then able to expand this new awareness beyond myself, to whomever or whatever I encountered. Going for rides on the city bus became one of my favourite places to put this new awareness into practice. Each time a new passenger would come onto the bus, the words God-Life, God-Love and God-Light would come to mind. They were God-Life, each and every one of them. Then, when I go for walks, or even at home while doing menial tasks, I like to breathe in God and then breathe out Love, Life or Light. While breathing in God and breathing out Love is a practice I had engaged in several years earlier, I was now able to truly feel it, but even more than that, I wanted to be with it. By engaging in this practice, I remain connected to Source/God, or Pure Life.

Now that the words God, Heaven, and Father no longer bother me, a whole new world has opened up. Whenever I read *A Course in Miracles*, or any other spiritual text, I don't choke on the words. I simply appreciate the message. Then I smile. I understand what is being said, no matter the language. Religious terminology doesn't bother me anymore, as I now see beyond the words, without the burden of ancient programming, just by the feeling. God is an experience. God is Life—Pure, all-encompassing, Loving Life. It includes every being, every thing, every aspect of creation. After learning to love oneself, another essential step on this journey may very well be reknowing God.

God is the initial spark expressing itself; it is Pure Life in natural, harmonious expression, with all of its potentialities, all of what it contains. Seeking to experience and know itself, it expands, manifests, grows, experiments, renews, discovers, and develops. It thus creates infinite expressions. Life is always in movement, expression, expansion and exploration as it is motivated by a desire to know itself. In Source there is—and always will be—the fundamental attributes of balance, harmony, inclusiveness, nurturing, love and light.

All of creation is an expression of Source, and so it is that everything is an aspect of this one Life Source. All creations emanating from Source are composed of aspects of its very own substance, and they too continue to grow and expand to experience and know themselves. At its origins, Pure Life is perfectly balanced. As its creations, we have the same attributes of creativity, curiosity, discovery, movement, expansion and expression. And so it is that we are far more than what we have, up until now, believed and known ourselves to be.

While I felt that I had finally truly made peace with God, I still had one tiny question. It wasn't something that would limit my experience; it was just a matter of curiosity. So, here it was: Who created God? I knew that I was pondering the imponderable, not really expecting an answer, but still, I was curious. Who created God?

I was walking home after running errands at the grocery store. It was a beautiful summer day, the sky was blue and clear and a light breeze brushed against my face. Although cars and trucks were buzzing noisily alongside me on the busy street as I neared my home, somehow nothing could remove the peace I felt. On a whim, I asked the question again: Who created God?

My attention was drawn in front of me, up high, into the clear blue sky, way past the horizon, beyond the furthest frontiers of time and space to an immense cloud of pure, soft, effervescent white light energy. As I watched, there emerged from the cloud of light the scant outline of a gentle, smiling, loving face. Then a pair of outstretched arms, palms wide-open, lovingly reached out to me.

Who created God? With a sweet, gentle gaze, the light form took a slow step back, almost like a dance step. Hmmm, I wondered. With that warm, loving smile and inviting arms outstretched, it took another long step back, and then another. Oh. Then I got it. God does not have a Creator; God is infinite. God has no beginning and no end. God is Pure Life. God is All That Is. God is. Period.

"And don't even try to understand this," my Guides told me, or more like teased me. "Just know it, reach up to it and embody its beautiful, loving energy." Which is exactly what I did. And now, when I recall this experience, I am overwhelmed by the loving embrace of the Source of Life, the All That Is—the smiling, kind, warm, loving embrace of God. Who wouldn't be! And I take a very deep breath and remember: God-Life; God-Love; God-Light.

CHAPTER 5

Once Upon a Time

[I]t is time to gather and integrate the lost parts of yourself.... Recognizing your own divinity feels like coming home; it awakens in you old memories of a blissful oneness and harmony you once knew. This is the miracle of the New Era: to be one and as one, to be a unique and individual consciousness and at the same time to be One with and connected to the whole. (*The Jeshua Channelings*, p. 120)

Is That All There Is?

Who am I? What am I? Why am I here? What is my purpose in this life? Could I be doing better? Is there more to life? Does it have to be so difficult? These are some of the questions many are asking today. The song "Is That All There Is?" performed by Peggy Lee expresses this so well. Inspired by Thomas Mann's short story "Disillusionment" written in 1896, the feelings of hopelessness, the despair and the deep sadness it expresses are not new. This incredibly beautiful, albeit sad song holds a belief we have carried for a long time—far too long—that all we can do is dance our way through life while making the best of it. If we can make it look good, if life isn't too hard, then we've done okay, perhaps even very well. But, is that truly all there is?

While writing this section, I couldn't help but mute the Classical station, turn on my speaker and dig out the song from my playlist. Just a suggestion: should you decide to give it a listen, grab a tissue or two. In case you're wondering if I cried, of course I did. When that song was first released, I was in my mid-teens, asking the same question, and so many more. Is that all there is, I wondered? It can't be, I remonstrated. Born a seeker of truth, I had already begun my journey, and the quiet, inner rebel in me wanted answers. Something in that child wouldn't settle for making a life as I was being taught it should be. There had to be more—had to be.

As I was writing these words, actually, more like staring at the words and trying to write, I listened to the song a few more times, and of course, the tears flowed. I shed those tears for the child in me who, well over half a century earlier, despite not seeing any light and unable to feel joy or hope, did not give up. It wasn't an easy journey back then for a young seeker. Without any support from family or friends, and without any way of connecting with others on the journey, she sought answers in traditional teachings. But, given that she was looking for a new way for humanity, those teachings did not quite answer her questions nor did they provide timely solutions. All I know is that she was a brave soul. She could have quit; she had opportunities to leave this life, and she had even contemplated it, but she stuck it out and for that, I love her dearly.

The more I think of it, the more I am convinced that the first step—loving oneself—is probably the single, most important step each and every one of us can take on this journey. Again, take a moment now and recall an incident from your past, a traumatic event or a challenging situation, a time when hope was lost. See that child or perhaps even the grown man or woman struggling and trying to make good, despite the difficulties or the mistakes, and just give that one a huge, loving hug. Feel the love. Love is not a word; love is meant to be felt. Only then can it be real. It is only when you feel it that you can truly know it. Set aside the circumstances and simply feel that love for yourself, know it now. Loving oneself—truly loving oneself—needs to be at the top of the list as we embark on this transition to a new way of Being.

When I asked for guidance as to why I had not really known love or had not been surrounded by love throughout most of my youth, the answer was so that I would know what it felt like, so I would know, firsthand, what so many humans on the planet have experienced throughout history, but also are still experiencing today. It was a sacrifice of sorts, but in a way, a necessary one, because if you do not know something from experience it can be very hard to feel compassion, to understand and relate to others. But first and foremost, it had been a necessary experience for my own healing, as there was still a part of me that believed that I was not worthy of love, especially the love of God.

Given the nature of the current human condition, most souls on the planet do not really know true love, let alone self-love. Much of the love expressed is conditional, meaning that it will be given if certain conditions are met. I love you because… I will always love you if…. The unconditional love humanity now needs to know is beyond what has commonly been experienced as it requires a conscious reconnection with our Source, Pure Life or God. This reconnection naturally requires the forgiving of past errors, the abandonment of who and what we think we are, and a willingness to know one's True Self. It is then not surprising that this became one of the greatest lessons of my life: the importance of loving oneself.

I also came to understand that for some souls, especially those who lived through hard times such as wars and economic collapse, motivated by intense fear and lack, love may have been set aside as the meeting of basic survival needs became a priority. When fear ruled and hope was lost, it may have seemed appropriate or even wise to stand up and be strong, reasonable and rational at the cost of feelings or emotions. Life was difficult, challenges needed to be overcome and there certainly was no place for weakness. Since love was seen as an emotion, at least the conditional love as experienced in the human condition, it may have been pushed back a little, or completely set aside, depending on the perceived need for strength. These souls did their best given their circumstances, and above all, given their understanding of who and what they believed themselves to be at the time.

After spending the better part of an afternoon listening to that touching song and wiping away tears, finally, I smiled. A great sense of relief, joy and peace came over me thanks to another dose of my favourite medicine: music. The next day, I was even able to listen to the song without any tears. What further lifted me up was the fact that what we have been learning over the past couple of decades clearly shows us that no, this is most definitely not all there is. There is much more—so much more!

Because many have asked, we are receiving answers. I am so very grateful for all those souls who have asked if that's all there is to life, those who were bold enough to wonder if there might be more. Also, if we have asked, it must be that something inside of us feels or even just suspects that we might be more than what we think we are or can ever imagine ourselves to be. That being so, it means that a far greater experience awaits us as we step forward through the Gateway to a new humanity. We are expressions of Pure Life, beings of Love and Light and unending creativity. We are, each and every single one of us, aspects of an infinite, creative, loving Life Source, simply waiting to grab that moment when we can once again reclaim and remember who and what we truly are.

In the Moment

Okay, but if this is true, if we really are, each and every one of us, aspects of an infinite, creative, loving Life Source, then why are we not living that glorious life filled with Love, Light and unending creativity, and maybe even some peace, abundance, and joy for all? You don't have to look too far to see that this world is not filled with Love and Light; quite the contrary. As an impatient person by nature, or maybe because I'm a tired, old seeker, I like to get to the root cause of a situation or problem.

I say "old" seeker because a few years ago, I had a flash of a past life a long time ago where I saw myself walking downhill, leaving behind a monastery, high up in the Himalayas. It seems that in that lifetime, I had grown impatient with the teachings, and as I wasn't learning what I felt I needed, I left. I had to chuckle when I learned of this, as I was not one bit surprised. It certainly fit the pattern of behaviour I had carried forward into this lifetime. It also explained why I was born in a female body, rather than in a male body. I have no doubt that if I had been born male, I would have headed straight for that Cistercian monastery and followed in the footsteps of Thomas Merton. It also explained my fascination for the book *Lost Horizon* by James Hilton when I was a teen.

Interestingly, that past life memory was later confirmed in a session with Daniel Scranton and the Arcturians. This confirmation was very helpful as it strengthened my trust and confidence in my inner knowing, in those tiny, seemingly insignificant flashes of insight and knowledge, those strange memories from the past that seemed to pop up out of nowhere. While I never actively sought out these memories, they nevertheless come at the right moment, usually providing insights for better understanding, learning or healing. As we are moving into what appears to be unknown territory, now, more than ever, we must learn to trust that inner voice, no matter how strange it may sound. This is something each and every one of us needs to do as we move forward into a new experience for humanity and begin to create a new world: turn inward for answers.

What I have found on this long journey is that much of the content found in traditional teachings doesn't quite give us the answers we need, at least not what is useful during this particular time of transition. Plus, I'm not a fan of complicated games, deciphering ancient secret codes and teachings, or engaging in fancy rituals. Why does it matter what happened a few thousand years ago on Earth when life dates back to eternity and out into many dimensions, beyond anything we can even comprehend? Plus, where have these teachings taken us?

Furthermore, while digging into our ancient history may be fascinating, or more likely overwhelming and confusing because of its overabundance, there is no consensus as to the accuracy of the information, nor is there any way of verifying its accuracy. So, at this time in particular, if we desire a new experience for humanity, perhaps we shouldn't spend too much time dillydallying with anything but the root cause. Examining the past is only useful if it helps us avoid repeating past mistakes and helps liberate us in the present moment.

So, I was quite happy when my Guides reminded me, once again, to forget the past.

"Let's put that impatience to good use," they added.

Put that impatience to good use? That was news to me! It made me sound less faulty, less defective. How about "God use"? Now that sounds good!

"Forget the historical Jesus. We are here now. You were right in your youth to want to look forward rather than to look back. You had an instinct; you had inner knowledge of a great leap that humanity was going to make in the future. The future is now. It's time for all of you to release the past. Yes, learn from it, look at it and then forgive it, let it go, and start creating a new future now."

"Thank you for that," I replied. So, what needs to be done is to forgive and let go. While this sounds simple, it may not be easy. The past is maintained as long as we believe we need it to inform the present. In fact, that is its sole purpose. As we forgive and release it, the past can be transformed. Things will remain as they are as long as we cling to our past stories and narratives to define, validate or substantiate our current positions. As we express our sincere desire and readiness, and above all, gather up the courage to move forward and embrace the new, to rise above the tired, old, limiting human condition, this need to cling to the past will be released, and eventually fade away. It will then be easier to heal whatever may be hindering our progress. Without a doubt, another one of our greatest tools during this transition period is forgiveness. To forgive and let go of the past is not only healing, it is also totally liberating and empowering.

I also understood that some of the attributes we have ascribed to our ancient teachers such as Jesus, the Buddha, our angel helpers, and others, are based on our limited understanding of the nature of life at the time they interacted with us on Earth. Since that time, they may very likely have transformed to much higher levels of who and what they are given that Life is always in a process of learning, growth and expansion. Also, we too have grown, so we can expect that the teachings being offered today might be different from what was provided ages ago. That being so, when asking for guidance from an ancient teacher, it may be helpful to release any long-held conceptions or beliefs about them and their teachings, since at this time, they may no longer apply. It is most appropriate to be open to entirely new perspectives, especially since we do not want to repeat the old. Again, this requires that we trust our inner voice, that inner channel of wisdom.

If, for example, you see Jesus as the one and only holy chosen son of God the Father who came here to save you, and you are sitting around waiting for him to come down and save you, you may want to reconsider your position. My early childhood understanding was of a man nailed to a cross with blood dripping down his face, hands and chest. It didn't look like he could save anyone, never mind me, since I was a girl, and besides, God preferred his special chosen son above anyone else. Plus, that father who loved him left him there to sacrifice himself and suffer for our sins. Oye! That persona didn't work for me.

Instead, I chose to see Jeshua as the man walking among the people—a gentle, loving, kind soul, ready to serve in any way he could, but especially, ready to teach his message of love, forgiveness and unity. This is probably why I love to go out for walks and chat with strangers along the way, or go on bus rides, or stroll through the grocery store aisles and chat with whoever needs a little love or laughter. I know I am not alone as my Guides walk alongside me.

Jeshua came to Earth during the transition between the Eras of Aries and Pisces with an essential message of love and unity. Using the language of the time, he taught that God the Father was the Creator of all, not just some special chosen group. As we entered the Era of Pisces, the attribute of boundless diversity was highlighted on Earth, a fascinating and unique experience that may not necessarily be found in other dimensions or galaxies. Universality, unlimited diversity and variety, as well as infinite possibilities are basic attributes of Pisces. And so it was only natural that the love of all and the love for all would be an essential element of the teaching of that new Era.

As it turned out, humanity was not quite ready for the messages Jeshua—and others—came to share. Instead, churches were instituted in his name, and his teachings were edited and modified so they could best suit the structures of the day. Given the low consciousness of those on Earth at the time, these teachings were integrated into the control systems used by those in power. While there are a few souls who maintained the truth as it was seeded in ancient religions, cultures, philosophies, traditions or spiritualities, these were not typically encouraged or even allowed to be shared. If the truth were to come out and love and oneness were to be adopted and lived by the masses, those in power would unavoidably become disempowered. It is only by maintaining a culture of divisiveness, the age-old divide-and-conquer weapon, that a very small group can have control over a very large group.

Given that humans had long forgotten the truth of who and what they are, they were not equipped, nor ready, to embrace a universal experience of love and unity. Instead, the Era of Pisces evolved—or perhaps devolved—into an Age of extreme divisiveness based on economic and social standing, culture, race, beliefs, gender and faith. This way of life was then sustained through the establishment of extensive control measures, hierarchies, competition, fear, indifference, cruelty and ever-present threats of war—the very opposite of the love, unity and inclusiveness which that Era held as a potential for life on Earth.

Much of this war, violence and competition had been carried forward from the previous Era of Aries. Without the integration of the principles of harmony, love, unity and the oneness of all of creation, mankind was unable to release the past and rise above those ancient practices. It is then not surprising that they were carried into the Era of Pisces; and here they are now, at our doorstep, awaiting our decision as to what we will do as we enter the new Era of Aquarius. Do we want to continue with the old? Or do we want something completely new?

Another key factor as we move forward is that when we release long-held conceptualizations of our past as well as definitions of who and what we think we are, fear, worry, shame, guilt, anger, hatred, resentment—any non-loving sentiments—will most likely rise to the surface. This will be our opportunity to forgive and let go. Free of the clutches of a fixed, rigid timeline—which is actually a very small aspect of a multi-dimensional, infinite reality—we will heal ourselves of the ancient wounds we have carried through countless generations. In so doing, the creation of a new world will be facilitated.

We may then begin to have extraordinary experiences such as teleportation, extrasensory communication, inter-dimensional travel, and even travel into the future or the past. Perhaps we can release and heal the past and create a new history, in preparation for the new future we desire. In reality, the past is not fixed; it is only carried forward and maintained by us. Just ask a friend to share their experience of an event you both lived in the past. Very likely your perspectives on the experience will be different, and may even be completely contrary. This means that what we carry forward from the past varies from person-to-person. Likewise, the future is not predetermined; it is only wished for, desired, imagined or feared by us. Even if you try to fix the past, you are doing it in the present, and any change or transformation that may ensue will be experienced in the present. Neither the past nor the future is real. There is only Now. All is transcended in the moment, and so it is that all is possible in the moment. Plus, what is experienced Now is based on our present level of consciousness.

So, Who and What Are We?

We are living in a time when, while it may seem more difficult than ever to be here on Earth, it is easier than ever to make a massive shift of consciousness. What is making this much-needed shift possible and even easier is the high level of discomfort we are currently experiencing. "Why would discomfort be a good thing?" you might ask. "That sounds sadistic!"

While discomfort is not an essential component for the transition into the new Era, much less an attractive or desirable one, it seems that throughout the millennia, we have fallen into a deep, safe, relatively comfortable, familiar slumber of sorts, settling for a little dance here, maybe a fine glass of wine there, and not much more. And so the discomfort may be for some, even many, the main driver pushing us for answers and nurturing our desire for real change. Rather than being angry or distraught, perhaps we should be grateful for the challenges we are experiencing, as they may very well be the kick in the butt that is needed!

What we are now learning is truly mind-altering. Actually, consciousness-altering may be a more fitting term. True change only requires that we abandon everything we think we know about ourselves, about the world and beyond, and be ready to face the unknown. Abandon everything? That might be a problem, given that Aquarius especially likes to know, its primary keywords being "I know." Understandably, this new Era is also very much in sync with science. In fact, if anything will replace the traditional religions in the coming years, it will most likely be science. As blind faith will not be sustainable in Aquarius, whatever is being taught, or used as a metric or gauge of any kind, will need to be tested and validated. Moving forward, humanity will no longer be as susceptible to having the wool pulled over its eyes, as was the case throughout the last several millennia.

As living beings, emanating from an infinite Source of Life, we are integral parts of a multi-dimensional universe, the vastness of which is probably impossible to comprehend given our current level of consciousness. This much is now being confirmed by the science of the day. If this is not what we are experiencing, it is simply because we are unaware of the breadth and scope of who and what we are. It is not a punishment or a trial of any kind. It is simply the result of a lack of awareness, or a forgetting. As unique aspects of this infinite universe, each one of us has a unique role to play and an equally unique contribution to make. As we begin to integrate this knowledge, as we allow our awareness to expand and include more of our potential, we will be able to put our attention in a com-

CHAPTER 5 · ONCE UPON A TIME

pletely new, much more expansive direction as multidimensional, higher-consciousness beings.

So, I'm writing, and you're reading. You exist, and I exist. These are our experiences in the moment, although our "moments" are unique to each of us. We can probably agree on that point. We know, from firsthand experience, that we exist; no one needs to confirm that for us. But, do we really, truly know all there is to know about who and what we are, let alone where we came from? Think about this for a minute. Who are you? Why do you think that? Where did you get the definitions about who and what you are? Do you really think that's all there is to you? What if this wasn't you at all? What if you were far greater than what you think you are now? Apparently, we are no more our genes than we are our jeans! What we are is so far beyond DNA, genetics, ancestry and history that it is nearly impossible to comprehend.

Many years ago, actually, decades ago, during a meditation I imagined what it might be like if I cut off my right arm. I realized that I would still be me. Then I imagined what it might be like if I cut off my left arm too, and again, I realized I would still be me. Even if I cut off my legs I would still be me; while maybe damaged, I would still be me. And so I am not just the body. I must be something else. So, what am I then? Who is it that wants to know? These were big questions and, unfortunately, there were no satisfactory answers available at the time.

In The Beginning

As we agree that we exist, we can probably also agree that in the beginning, there is a Creator, Pure Life, a God or Source, the Word, an Infinite Life Principle, an original impulse, a spark, energy or Mind behind all of creation, or at least the creation of which we are a part. In other words, our universe had to start somewhere. Now, here is where it can get a little more complicated. In the original manifestation of Source, there must be elements that allow for growth, expansion and creativity such as curiosity, a desire to discover, to experience and know since creation is always in movement. However, while Source, or God, is creative, expressive and expansive by nature, it must also stand on a foundation of balance, peace, harmony, wisdom, unity and inclusiveness, as well as love and respect for all of its creations. One of its greatest attributes is very likely that it works in harmony, without divisiveness, competition or conflict of any kind. If this were not so, it would run the risk of harming itself or worse, it would set itself up for annihilation.

For all we know, the Creator may have occasionally stumbled in its countless creative expressions, unintentionally or accidentally overlooking its fundamental laws of harmony and balance, perhaps actually resulting in the non-functionality of some of its creations. Since the Source of All Life cannot be destroyed, these creations would simply have been recycled and then given new life. This may even have occurred many times. We just don't know. Since creation as we know it, as expressed in our world, our universe, is still in existence, it must be that its Creator, Source, or God, abides by these laws of unity, balance and harmony and no doubt other essential principles.

Furthermore, what Source, All That Is, or God creates must be like itself, or at least must contain some aspects or components of itself. Otherwise, how could it create something different from or other than itself if this Source, or God, is all there is? This means that everything that is from Source is infinite at its core and cannot be destroyed. Yet, that is not our experience as living beings on Earth, and perhaps even in other worlds or dimensions. Also, as each one of us is an aspect of creation, without one of us, creation would be incomplete. Together we embody Source or All That Is in expression. While each is unique, not one is less than or more than the other, as all are integral aspects of the whole. Yet, why is this not our experience?

So, we exist, and it appears that we are the result of an innate desire of Source or God to express and know itself, to grow, expand and discover Life. If this is true, how did we become so ignorant of our origins? How did we get to be so small, so powerless?

CHAPTER 5 · ONCE UPON A TIME

Why do we not know that we are expressions of a vast, balanced, harmonious, loving, creative, beautiful Source of all Life?

There are many different stories in our cultures, traditions and religions that attempt, or even claim, to answer these questions. Each person will need to choose the version that resonates with them, the perspective that helps them shift to the best level of awareness of who and what they are. If none of the traditional stories work, create your own. On this subject, as can be expected, there is no consensus, and that's okay, since each person's journey is unique. Where I personally have learned to draw the line and move on is when a story stands on a foundation of fear, exclusiveness, divisiveness, superiority, specialness, shame, guilt, judgment, condemnation or punishment. These traits do not reflect a balanced, all-inclusive, harmonious, loving God or Source, and so these stories cannot reflect the true God, at least not the God I have come to know. Again, each one will choose the line of thought that works for them.

The concept of being created in the image and likeness of God now becomes an interesting one and it has far greater implications than most people realize. Actually, it has far greater implications then many would actually be ready to accept. In light of what we are now learning, we can re-examine this ancient, rather confusing bit of dogma. How can we be created in the image and likeness of God? Everyone can't be created in the image and likeness of God! What about those humans doing horrendous things? They are not like God! Well, either all is of God, or it isn't. By its essential nature, Pure Life, Source, the Creator or God, creates and expresses, grows, expands and becomes more of itself. How could something that is perfect, whole and infinite create anything that is less than perfect? Does it make mistakes?

What follows is a story of creation that emerged out of my own musings, inspired by what I have read in many traditional and contemporary spiritual works, but also with the help of my Guides. I say with the help of my Guides because I feel their presence very strongly with regards to my writing. It appears that I am being guided to write about complex or unusual subjects in a way that is accessible and easy to understand for myself, but also so that the reader may in turn explore and experience these and other concepts for themselves. As each one undertakes their own journey of questioning and exploration, the shift of consciousness for humanity as a whole will be accelerated.

This story of creation is purely imaginary. It is not backed by science or rigorous testing, nor is it peer-reviewed or endorsed by a religious organization. It is simply a tale that helped me see humanity in a new light. All that matters is that it works for me, at least for now, or until a new perspective emerges. What works for us in the moment is what is most important and especially, helpful. Since what Pure Life or God creates is multidimensional and so far beyond that with which we are familiar, there is probably no way we could understand the starting point of creation. In a multi-dimensional context, our familiar linear timeline becomes basically irrelevant. However, we can imagine what might have led to the creation of humanity, if only to satisfy our curiosity and perhaps nurture our journey as we create a new world.

Once Upon A Time

In all my studies, I have never found a story of creation that was entirely satisfactory. Sure, there are lots of myths, metaphors and parables, but I'm a hands-on person. I'd rather go in the kitchen and figure out a new recipe for making seitan than try to figure out some vague mystical symbolism about the origins of life and how to fend off Satan. It is also reasonable to point out that given our current 3-D or 4-D level of perception, our comprehension of what is infinite is likely to be somewhat limited—more likely very limited. The true story of creation is nearly impossible to imagine on this level, at least for the non-questioning mind. However, if I had to make up a story of creation and the origins of life on Earth and very likely in other worlds too, that might make sense to me, it would go something like this:

CHAPTER 5 • ONCE UPON A TIME

From the original impulse of Creation, or Word, out of the infinite potentialities of Pure Life, Source or Mother/Father/God, there emerged conscious, living, "Divine Beings"—extensions of the Creator. These beings were made of spirit, mind, light, energies, frequencies and vibration that carried a desire to expand, explore, grow, learn and create. This was only natural as they were created in the image and likeness of God. The innate creative impulse of these Divine Beings was then naturally expressed outward into countless spaces and dimensions, manifesting as systems, galaxies, planets and life forms that would enable them to uncover, expand, explore and express their boundless creativity. Throughout all of these experiences, much was learned and innumerable skills and abilities were developed. All of these creations embodied the attributes of Source: balance, harmony, respect, inclusiveness, love, and so many more. Creation was an adventure, an opportunity to express that innate curiosity to discover All That Is and to play with and explore the infinite potentialities inherent in Pure Life.

Gifted with the freedom to choose how to express their creative energies, choices were constantly being made, most of which were beneficial for all life and contributed to the expansion and blossoming of Pure Life into infinite expressions. On occasion, some choices led to outcomes or creations that were not as beneficial. In other words, errors were made along the way—just errors—not sins, not intentionally perpetrated evil or crimes, just mistakes. As these beings embodied the balance, harmony, respect, wisdom, love and light attributes of their Creator, errors were immediately corrected, lessons were learned, and as needed, energies were recycled and life continued to expand and grow.

As these Divine Beings were experiencing life in a multidimensional way, they were not bound by a linear timeline. And so when corrections were made, past errors were simply released, lessons were learned, and a new present moment emerged. These Divine Beings, who may also be called sons and daughters of God, or children of God, would then continue to learn and discover and know themselves through their ever-expanding, ongoing experiences.

This was an exciting and joyful phase for all of creation, and especially for its Divine Creator Beings, for such is the nature of Pure Life in expression.

Eventually, some of the original creator beings became so captivated by, and even overly preoccupied with their creations that their essential connection to Source began to fade. In and of itself, that was not necessarily wrong, and it could easily be corrected with a simple reminder, or a little nudge from a Divine brother or sister, or a Guide. "Hey, you're way more than that! You're a Divine Being, remember? You belong to the family of All of Creation, the family of God." However, enamoured by their infinite potential and countless multidimensional experiences, these adventurous souls grew further and further apart from their Divine family. The reminders and gentle nudges did not quite reach them, or they were simply brushed aside as they desired to continue with their adventures. In time, the consciousness or awareness of being an integral part of a Whole, or an aspect of Oneness gradually diminished. Bit by bit, they forgot who and what they were as Divine Beings, expressions of a united, balanced, harmonious, nurturing, loving, creative Source.

As these adventurous souls continued to experiment on their own, independently from Source, or God, their creations in various galaxies and dimensions began to lose some of the inherently elevated frequencies of Pure Life. Less wholesome choices were made, resulting in a gradual decline or degradation of Pure Life to lower, denser, less enlightened dimensions of manifestation. Things began to go awry, and what was expressed lost some of its natural harmony, balance and essential sense of Oneness. This inevitably led to the lowering of consciousness of the beings involved, gradually causing the memory of their essential divinity to be completely eroded. While this occurred in many places throughout the multi-verse, it was particularly evident and powerful on the physical Earth plane.

As consciousness is reduced and diminished, the awareness of the Allness of Life fades. This is much like sliding the dimmer down on a light switch until there is no more light. In a less "enlightened" state of consciousness, visibility is reduced and awareness becomes more self-based than All-based, or more exclusive than inclusive. As deep-forgetting sets in, choices made may not necessarily be beneficial for all, or even for self. This was particularly the case as the original Creator Beings tumbled from the highest dimensions of consciousness holding infinite potentialities, to lower dimensions, which were increasingly densified, thus severely reducing and limiting potentialities.

Driven by their innate sense of curiosity and their desire to create and experience anything and everything they possibly could, these adventurous souls eventually found themselves in the lowest possible level of expression, the third dimension, or physical dimension, as is currently being experienced on Earth. The establishment of this lower consciousness experience was built up, expanded and firmly structured into something that became an all-encompassing reality for those choosing to have the experience. These souls grew more and more captivated by their new creation, until it became the only reality that was remembered, the only creation of which they were aware.

In the process, these inherently Divine Beings suffered the deep loss of connection with Pure Life, God, or Source of who and what they truly were as integral parts of a flowing, balanced, harmonious, infinite, creative reality. The experience of "duality" thus emerged as these adventurous souls now believed themselves to be separate and apart from their Creator. This exciting new sense of duality was then incorporated into their creations, manifesting an emphasis on outer versus inner, light versus dark, great versus small, abundance versus lack, which eventually was expressed as self versus non-self, or self versus other. This was a fascinating experience as it was completely different from what had been known in the state of Oneness of Pure Life.

The originally balanced yin/yang or male and female energies were also split so that some beings embodied the female while the others embodied the male energies. Once the physical dimension was firmly established as being separate from Source, it naturally followed that those souls who wanted to experience this level of life on Earth were required to embody through the joining of a sperm and an egg, the one remaining symbol of balance and unity between the male and female energies. This was very different from their prior experiences of having a thought or a desire to manifest somewhere in the multi-verse and simply appearing there. To experience life on Earth, physical incarnation was now required.

This process of moving away from unity with Source happened in ways that are almost impossible to conceptualize from the limited Earth-bound perspective. Yet, despite their stumbling errors and their forgetfulness, these Divine Beings will always remain what they truly are as expressions of Source or God, for nothing can harm or destroy what comes from Pure Life. Plus, nothing exists outside of Pure Life, or God.

These Beings were like a small bunch of very adventurous children who broke away from the group, leaving behind their siblings, friends and neighbours so they could wander off into an unknown part of the woods. At first they enjoyed the adventure, especially the sense of doing their own thing. They were faced with the need to fend for themselves, take care of their basic needs, and protect themselves and their meagre possessions. In the process, they learned to hone their unique skills. Some were good with foraging for berries under the bushes, while others found clean water in a nearby brook. A few were great at organizing the sharing and preservation of the berries, while others found ways for them to sleep on soft beds made of leaves under the shade of the trees. In time however, they had wandered so far off that they began to sense a deep, inner lack, a homesickness for which they had no remedy. Feeling lost and unable to find their way home, they grew fearful, and even began to fight among themselves for what they thought they needed. Having forgotten that they had freely made the choice to wander off into the forest, they began to look for someone or something outside themselves to blame for their feelings of loss, grief and fear.

It was only natural that such an experience of separation from family and community would lead to concerns over safety and survival. However, what the children forgot was that the forest was really a playground they had all created together, and the entire playground remained always surrounded by their homes. While playing their make-believe games, they also forgot that their less-adventurous family and friends, those who had decided not to follow them into the woods, remained always nearby, ready to help in any way they could, just waiting for them to come home.

Wanting to respect and honour their freedom of choice, those who had chosen to not join them in their adventure simply stood back and allowed them to learn from their experiences. They knew that in time, as all were Divine Creator Beings, they would remember who and what they are and realize that they had never really left home. Still, a couple of the brothers and sisters found it difficult to stand by and watch the adventurous ones struggle, and so they decided to step in and try to help. However, having completely forgotten who they really were and where they came from, the adventurous souls were so frightened by the forms that appeared before them that they ran away and hid. "I saw a ghost! There was an evil spirit! Run!"

Not wanting to further frighten them, the helpers stepped back and agreed to wait patiently. They knew that at any moment their adventurous brothers and sisters could simply stand up and look beyond the boundary of their playground and remember exactly who and what they are. Besides, they knew very well that despite their forgetting, they would always remain Divine expressions of God, manifestations of Pure Life. All they needed was to be curious enough to ask: Is that all there is? This would reignite the Divine Creator spark that resides always in their hearts—that resides in all hearts—and they could then begin their journey Home.

So it is with all humans on Earth at this time. Throughout thousands and thousands of years there did not appear to be an alternative. Until now. We are now learning differently. Our Creator Self, the Divine in us that knows the Truth, along with our brothers and sisters, our family of Divine Creator Beings, extend their hands, inviting us to stand tall and remember, claim and realize once again our true Divine nature. "No, that's not all there is! You are so much more than this small self you have believed yourselves to be for far too long! It's time for you to remember who and what you are," they say, with loving, open arms, ready to embrace us and welcome us back into the Oneness of Life. "We welcome you Home now. Come Home now!"

> The law of creation is that you love your creations as yourself because they ARE part of you... You are at home in God, dreaming of exile, but perfectly capable of awakening to reality. (ACIM, Ch. 9, p. 221)

Your Story of Creation

As each one's journey is unique, the reader is invited to create their own story of creation in a language that is as free as possible of past definitions and concepts so that it can help establish a clear path for the future. We invite you here to use your imagination to make up your own story, your own version of the origin of life on Earth or perhaps even the entire multi-verse. Now that sounds foolish, you might say, in view of the fact that no one really knows the full story of creation. And you would be right, since the vastness of creation is far beyond human understanding or even simple conceptualization. However, everyone has a version of the story of creation that they believe in, a story they cling to because that is what they were taught in school, or in church, or through a cultural heritage. Whether it's the Big Bang theory—note that this is just a theory—or the myth of Creation by the hand of an all-powerful, all-knowing, judging, punishing God—again, just a myth—everyone believes in something. The important point here is to pay attention to how the story you hold, the story you are accustomed to, makes you feel.

For example, perhaps your version of the story of creation makes you feel indifferent, like you couldn't care less about what happened since it was just a mechanical or quantum event that happened so long ago that it doesn't directly affect you. In such a case, you probably would not be interested in reaching out to know more about your origins, to discover the more of who, and what you might be. This perspective may even make you feel cold, isolated, further alienating you from your origins. Who cares; it happened such a long time ago. We're here now; let's just live our best life.

If your story of creation makes you fearful of encountering a mythical judging, punishing, critical, all-powerful God, here again, you may not feel drawn to meeting this Creator Source. I'm just going to do my best, follow the rules, and hope that there will be a place for me in Heaven when I die. I've made mistakes in my life; I'm not ready for that punishment. So there is no need for me to rush out and meet God before my time.

These stories of our origins, whether cultural, historical, religious, or science-based serve as the structure or foundation for our life experiences on Earth. Whatever story you cling to colours your vision of what is, as well as of what might be. So, why not make up a story that makes you curious, that makes you want to know and experience more, a version of the story of creation that makes you eager to discover your true origins as an expression of Pure Life, God-Life, God-Love, God-Light. Use language that is free of past ideologies and definitions. Create a new story, one that will support the creation of a new future for life on Earth. Let your story bring you hope, joy, peace, and an unending feeling of being loved. Give it a try, and see how it makes you feel. Building and relying on your own unique perspective is entirely appropriate in the Era of Aquarius. In fact, it is one of its essential attributes.

> Just as you are now confronted with many schools of thought, so, too, was I [Jeshua]. And while that can seem to lead to great confusion, as though one must choose from the smorgasbord, it actually serves not unlike the sand inside the oyster from which the pearl will come. It causes you to grate inside. *You must find your own way to your own truth.* For before each and every one of you lies your pathway and a doorway, an eye of the needle, through which *only you* can fit. (*The Way of the Heart*, Lesson 4)

Vision of a New World

What would a new world look like?
Healing for everyone
An end to physical and mental health illnesses
Abundant joy and laughter
Greeting each new day with enthusiasm
Love shared all around
A wonderful community spirit
Inspiration for everyone
Harmony in all things
Peace, yes deep peace that never leaves
The beauty of music and art
A respect and care for nature
Working at things you love to do
Love in every heart
Heaven on Earth!

Michael J. Miller

CHAPTER 6

Finding Hope

The Soul has not only been fully created, but has also been created perfect. (ACIM, Ch. 2, p. 21)

So Much More

Okay, we now have a new story—our own story—a new myth of creation, one that is probably quite different from what we were taught. At any rate, it's a story that resonates with us, one that may even inspire us and ignite our curiosity to know more and to move forward on this great journey of discovery that is our life. But it's still just a story!

True but, isn't most of what we think and believe, actually, isn't all of our life based on some kind of story? The fact is that our entire existence is founded on a wide range of stories from the story of creation to our personal, family, social and cultural histories. Everything we do is tainted by what we have learned, and what we have learned is based on stories from our history, heritage, culture and traditions which very often hold a bias. For example, who wrote the stories of our wars and great battles? The winners or the losers? The conquerors or the conquered? Who wrote the stories of our ancient history? The nobility or the slaves? Many of our stories appear to carry happy or satisfactory endings. But happy or satisfactory for whom? Furthermore, most of our collective narratives serve to dictate how we should live our lives. This is how it's always been done, so this is how I should do it. But again, who does this serve?

Using our new story of creation as a backdrop, we can now ask ourselves if what we have always done is the best we can do. Has it brought out our highest potential? Is it healing our deepest, ancient wounds? Is it helping us dare to step up and help create a new world? Could there be more grace, harmony, inclusiveness, compassion, love and respect for all life on Earth?

What we experience as individuals today is also based upon our past, on how we recall events that occurred years ago, or even on what we did yesterday. The next time you go shopping with a friend, at the end of the day, ask them to share their experience of the outing. Maybe it was a lovely summer day, a weekday when the mall was not overly crowded. Very likely you will have shared similar experiences; you both noticed the new sportswear store, or the closing of what was once a popular shoe store. But, you may also have had an experience that was unique to each of you.

Perhaps your friend was reminded of the last time she was shopping in that mall and found a wonderful Christmas gift for her grandson, a fire truck with a flashing light and beeping horn. That gift had made him so happy and excited that he had run to her and given her the biggest hug ever. That momentary recollection may have added an extra element of warmth and joy to the outing for your friend.

On the other hand, maybe you crossed paths with the neighbour from down the street who had phoned to inform you last spring that he had found your long-lost cat. Apparently, Bucky had fallen in his pool and drowned just before winter. For a minute or so, you felt a pinch in your heart as you recalled the loss of your beloved pet. So while you were sharing the same outing, on the same sunny summer day, your experiences were coloured by your past.

Since each person's experience carries a unique version of any event, why not create stories that help us heal, grow and rise to the more of who and what we are? Even if you hold onto the story for a very short time, as long as it can help you stand up and look for more without the burden of those long-held stories that inhibit your progress, healing and growth, it may be very helpful. It's okay to create stories that do not interest publishers and filmmakers; what is important is to create stories that uplift and inspire us. So it is that

CHAPTER 6 · FINDING HOPE

I'm being nudged once again to share some of my music stories. But first, a little background might be helpful to provide context. What follows is a tale I wrote in AARCT illustrating what it might be like for a group of aliens to visit Earth for the first time.

Imagine for a minute, maybe a couple of minutes—hey, why not turn it into a sci-fi movie?—imagine that you are overhearing a conversation coming from a group of aliens, highly enlightened beings from a galaxy far, far away. They have travelled to many places in this vast universe, but this is the first time they visit planet Earth. From the clearing in the woods where they landed, enveloped by a soft breeze, the sun shining warmly upon them, welcomed by the song of the birds chirping in the trees, they look around to gather a sense of how life has unfolded on this planet. Standing in awe, they all agree that this is truly one of the most beautiful planets of all the galaxies they have visited.

However, as our visitors begin to explore life on Earth, will their sense of awe be maintained? Will they be as impressed by our progress and evolution as we are?

As they begin their tour, the aliens first observe that the beings on this planet appear to be from one race—the human race. Like all expressions of Source, they are naturally connected and have the ability to share and communicate with one another. Together, they have the potential to express, manifest and experience wonderful things. Indeed, they appear to have tremendous knowledge, creative abilities, abundant resources and a wealth of ancient wisdom. They have so much to experience and so much to share! Clearly, this is a place where they must be thriving, learning and growing together as they care for each other and for the rich and bountiful planet that is their host. On such a beautiful planet, they conclude, humans should be doing rather well.

However, as our galactic visitors become more acquainted with life on Earth, they come to realize that, unfortunately, this is not what is being experienced by its inhabitants.

Humans live in a world deeply divided by anything and everything that might wedge them apart: beliefs, culture, land, politics, wealth, education, age, religion, language, status, gender and race. In this climate of divisiveness, they struggle, compete, even kill each other to survive and maintain their little spot of separateness on this planet. Beneath this struggle is the greatest fear of all: that their cherished possessions can be taken away in an instant.

"None of this is necessary," one visitor says to the others with a sad shake of the head. "If they only knew."

Feeling nothing but love for their Earthly brothers and sisters, the aliens ponder how humans could turn this dismal situation around and make this a better world for all—the world it was meant to be—the world it can now be. It would appear that humans have forgotten that each and every one is a member of this family of living beings, that all are expressions of the One loving Source. They have forgotten that at the centre of every single being resides the most powerful force of all—love. Without this essential sense of belonging and without love, humans cannot grow and rise to their full potential, either as individuals or as a united humankind.

Our wise visitors know that since each being is free to choose their experience, and each contributes to the experience of the whole, humans will need to choose differently if they want to manifest something different on Earth. If they would only be still a while, learn to breathe deeply and release the resistance and the struggles, choose peace instead of fear, turn their attention inward and reconnect with who and what they truly are, they would know how to turn the tide and rise to their greatest potential.

As our alien friends prepare to end their tour of planet Earth, they pause at the edge of a park where the townsfolk have gathered for an outdoor summer concert. Standing next to a sweetly scented flowering bush behind the last row of chairs,

CHAPTER 6 · FINDING HOPE

they listen in awe while the orchestra and choir perform Beethoven's "Ode to Joy." They all agree that humans are indeed capable of so much more—so, so much more.

"But," one of the aliens ponders while wiping away a tear, "are they ready to do whatever it takes to bring about this much-needed change?"

"Let us pray that they are ready and willing and courageous enough to do so," another replies. "We will always remain available to help in any way we can, should they reach out." (AARCT, Ch. 5, pp. 63-64)

One day, several months after the publication of the book, while I was working at the computer, Beethoven's 9th started to play on my usual classical station. When the piece reached the 4th movement, a couple of minutes before the choir section started I felt drawn to the living room where the music was playing. There I stood, in front of the television, until, all of a sudden, I raised my arms and began to move them up and down, across and sideways, fingers coming together between phrases, as though I was conducting an orchestra. It was like I was painting a canvas of music in the air. Again, keep in mind that I am just a beginner piano student, and this old body can only take so many hours at a keyboard. The best I can do is simple versions of "Fly Me to the Moon," "Fields of Gold" and "Scarborough Fair," so I didn't understand any of this.

As the choir joined the orchestra, I burst into tears. I cried. I cried so hard for humanity. I saw humanity's potential, how we could all be working together as one family, with compassion, understanding, wisdom and light. While I wasn't aware of the meaning of the lyrics, I felt drawn to pray for the healing of humanity. Once the piece was finished, I remembered the tale I had written about aliens visiting Earth and their experience of Beethoven's 9th. It was as though I had written it as a preview of my own experience. Or, perhaps that tale had sowed the seed for my experience. I had no idea of what was going on. All I knew was that now I was the one crying for humanity, not just the imaginary aliens.

A few weeks later, I found myself once again, in front of the television, but this time it was my favourite piece, Rachmaninoff's Piano Concerto No. 2. Within seconds, my arms, hands, and fingers were painting that beautiful music in the air. As I stood there, conducting an invisible orchestra, it felt as though someone had taken over my body, and of course, I was crying, crying and crying, especially during that most powerful last movement where he just drives it home. I had learned about the importance of letting in the feelings, of letting go of emotions, but this was so overwhelmingly powerful that it didn't make any sense.

When I asked my guides to help me understand what had happened, the answer was: "It's your future self." Wow! I had read in *The Jeshua Channellings* where Jeshua describes how his future self had helped him while in his life on Earth, and also in *Heart Centred Living*, where he invites us to reach out and get in touch with our future self. But I never expected to have that kind of experience myself. And my future self would be a musician? A monk, yes, but a musician? That was so weird. This happened once again, a few months later, same piece, same takeover, and again, I was stunned by the intensity of whoever I or that person was.

And so my guides shared the following: "In your future life, you will teach young people about Classical music." Wow! Many times I have said that it is a shame how young people today do not get to experience this beautiful music. I could very easily see myself as a teacher of music, so I happily agreed with that bit of information. "Now, go write," they added, and I knew they were smiling. And so I returned to writing.

Okay, so it seems that it is possible for us to connect not only with our past self, or selves, but also with our future self. From what I have learned, it may also be possible to connect with aspects of ourselves that exist in dimensions that are not bound by the materiality of the linear timeline. We certainly have much to discover and learn! Given the current state of the world, in a way, those glimpses of a possible future self—especially as a musician—shed a great ray of hope on a horizon that seemed to be tainted by nothing but dark

CHAPTER 6 · FINDING HOPE

hopelessness. It was nice to know that there would be life on Earth in the future, that humanity was not headed for annihilation.

Guess what concert I had attended the night before I started working on this chapter? Are there ever any accidents? Did I cry at that concert? Surprisingly, although I was moved, and my eyes were watery, there were no fountains of tears. I was prepared; I had a tissue up each sleeve. However, while the performance of Beethoven's 9th was very beautiful, I was not torn apart as I had been recently. Why was that? Had I lost my sensitivity, was my compassion failing?

"No, not at all," I was reassured. Apparently, while I might always shed a few tears—okay, maybe quite a few—when listening to a beautiful piece of music, there was no longer any need to cry out of despair, from an age-old dark place of desolation and hopelessness. Much of the pain I had harboured over lifetimes of struggle on Earth had been released through those tears. I had also learned, finally, that we have the answers we need now, and so I had found hope. Yes, we are more, and yes, we are capable of so much more, but the best part is that we are now learning how to become the more of who and what we are. Plus, we are being given the tools, the keys to that knowledge, and for those who have the courage to claim it and put some of this into practice, the sky is the limit or, if you prefer, the Kingdom of Heaven is at hand. Clearly, it is our time, now.

> Every tear releases burdens that have been carried for lifetimes, and it is not even necessary to know what those burdens are, to bring them up and to label them and to categorize them again; that would only tie them to you longer. But as you release them in the free flowing of the fountain of tears, they are gone forever. (Jeshua Online—Daily Message)

Thank you Judith and Jeshua. Thank you.

The Big Breakup

Okay, so let's say we have made space for a story that inspires us to let go of the past, explore the more of who and what we are, and perhaps even gives us hope. How does that help us now? It's still just a story! Although our new myth of creation may establish a foundation of infinity and wholeness and all sorts of good stuff for all life, that's obviously not what we are experiencing here on Earth at this time. Plus, we are most definitely not perfect, let alone Divine Infinite Beings. We are born, we live our lives as best we can, we get old and then we die. So, as the beautiful, heart-wrenching Marvin Gaye song goes, What's going on? Why is this infinity stuff not our experience? Who is pursuing this stuff anyway? Certainly not my family, my neighbours or even my close friends. This all sounds like a bunch of foolish spiritual, New Age nonsense. Just look at the world!

In case you were wondering, yes, I did listen to "What's Going On" while working on this section and again while editing it, and yes, the tears flowed. How could they not? It was my favourite album back in the day. Over 50 years later, we're still asking the same question. What's going on? Even young people listening to it for the first time are moved to tears as they sense there is something wrong with the current condition of life on Earth. When I learned about this, again, I felt hope. Young people were questioning. That was good. That was great! We need to give up the brutality, the judgment, the hatred, the condemnation and bring in the love we so desperately yearn for.

It is true that not everyone will be interested in pursuing this quest to uncover the path to a new world, or for a new experience for humanity or even for themselves. There are those who are having a pretty good life, or at least an okay life. As long as life doesn't throw them a curve ball or things don't get too much out of hand, they are not likely to be interested in seeking for more or making significant changes in their life. Life's good; why change it? Then there are those who are just too caught up in the busyness of everyday life; there's just no time. Understandably, this journey is not likely for them either, at least not for now. They can jump in at any time. And, as we will see, that's perfectly okay since each one's path is uniquely designed to meet their needs.

However, there is a growing number of souls on Earth at this time who are not satisfied with their lives, who are tired of the constant challenges, the struggles and the difficulties. Nor are they thrilled with what is going on in the world. For some, it all seems hopeless. It doesn't matter if they go to church every week, meditate, pray every day, or read all the latest spiritual or New Age books, nothing seems to help. How can we fix this? What can we do? Nothing works! I think it's time to leave!

As we know, we can't fix a problem on the level of the problem. Personally, I like simple, hands-on solutions, something I can actually work with, something that won't take thousands of lifetimes to achieve, unlike what I was taught half a century ago as a member of a local group of "initiates." That bit of teaching alone certainly set me back a couple of years. It took a while for me to release the disheartening idea that it would take that long to rise above my current limited level of human experience. Fortunately, in time I learned that the quickest way to solve a problem is to go straight to the root cause. And the quickest way to get to the root of the problem of the human condition is to head straight to the origins of life, where it all started in the first place. With our new—albeit hypothetical—story of creation, this becomes much easier.

Let us start with the premise that the original impulse of Pure Life, Source, Divine Creator Energy, or Mother/Father/God is naturally balanced, wise, curious, creative, harmonious, supportive, respectful, inclusive, caring, compassionate, nurturing and loving. As it is founded on a solid basis of Oneness, on a principle of Unity, it cannot be dualistic, and so it does not engage in battle, divisiveness, segregation, judgment, punishment, vindication, vengeance or competition of any kind otherwise it would harm, damage or even destroy itself. Even the male and female, or yin and yang energies, which are each unique and essential attributes of the Life Principle, work in a balanced and harmonious way, and together, they contribute to the unfolding and expansion of creation. While this perspective remains hypothetical and has not yet been scientifically proven, at least it's something I can work with. In due time, science will no doubt come to the same or similar conclusions, but there is no need to wait decades or centuries for scientific proof. We can get to work now.

> To accept yourself as God created you cannot be arrogance because it is the DENIAL of arrogance. To accept your littleness IS arrogant because it means that you believe YOUR evaluation of yourself is TRUER than God's. (ACIM, Ch. 9, p. 219)

The claim that what Source, or God, creates must be like itself, may not be easy to accept, at least not at first. It means that that's the stuff of which we are made. This must be so because Source cannot create anything that is other than itself since there is nothing that is other than or outside of Source. Basically, Pure Life is All That Is, so everyone and everything we encounter is an expression of this Source and carries traits of this Source. For most, this point may seem a bit difficult to digest, but it cannot be overemphasized. Maybe it sounds nice, at least in theory, or maybe it sounds arrogant; either way, it certainly is not what we are experiencing here on Earth. Why is that?

If this is true and it is not what we are experiencing, then what we are experiencing must not be real, or at least not entirely real. If we are experiencing something other than what Source is expressing, something that does not reflect the inherent attributes of Source, it must mean that we are experiencing an illusion or a dream, our own made-up version of reality, or what some call the "matrix" or a simulation. It's like a group of children creating a town with their Lego blocks. That's just about how real our experience is here on Earth and very likely on other planets and in other dimensions as well. These creations cannot be entirely real since they are missing essential components of Pure Life such as inclusiveness, balance, unity, harmony and love.

CHAPTER 6 · FINDING HOPE

This makes sense if we accept that we are created in the image and likeness of God, meaning that, at our core, we are essentially Divine, Creator Beings. In our story of creation, we saw how the original Divine Beings, or sons and daughters of God, were free to play with the talents and gifts naturally inherent in them as extensions of Source such as spirit, light, love, desire, curiosity, creativity—providing an endless ocean of potentialities. Using their fundamental creator impulses to explore, discover, grow, learn and expand, they built galaxies, worlds and communities—all filled with infinite possibilities.

At first, they lived and worked in peaceful, joyful, abundant and wholesome harmony. They thrived, grew and learned in their communities, while maintaining the utmost of respect for each other and for the galaxies and planets on which they chose to express and experience life. This was how life was meant to be lived for beings that knew themselves as integral aspects of the Whole, in what has likely been referred to as the "Garden of Eden," or perhaps the "Kingdom of Heaven."

However, like the children in our tale who became lost while playing in the forest, some of the more adventurous souls wondered if it might be possible to live outside of the Oneness of Source, and so they chose to leave the Garden of Eden just to give it a try. This bold adventure, fostered by innate curiosity, led to the abandonment of their inherent connection to Source, or the denial of God. Increasingly absorbed in and distracted by their experiments as independent creators, these souls eventually lost the memory of their origins. Once disconnected from their Source, or living in denial of God, they forgot the laws of creation and experimented in countless ways, using some attributes here, some attributes there. However, because they were not functioning in a state of Oneness or unity with All, things got out of balance. While they may not have been aware of their innate Divine Creator abilities, they had not entirely lost them. So it is that they were still able to create alternate worlds, or fantasies, or make-believe universes without the essential attributes of Pure Life.

As their adventure into independence progressed, a deep, very real sense of separation from Source was established. As a result, they forgot that one is always a part of the Whole, that God, the original Creator, is All That Is and that Oneness cannot be broken into bits and pieces nor can it be abandoned. Functioning now as separate, individual entities, or at least pretending as though it were even possible, they overlooked some of the core attributes that would naturally be expressed if they had remained connected to Source such as harmony, inclusiveness, balance, community, respect, compassion and love. Any expression of the universe or creation that appears to, or attempts to function independently from Pure life or God can only be imagining or making something up, since Creation must function in a united, harmonious, balanced way.

In time, after having generated the "big bang" of separation from Source or, after having "pulled the plug" from the Infinite Life Source, these independent adventurous souls began to rely more and more on their thinking apparatus. They created language to which meaning was attributed. This method of information gathering and sharing eventually replaced the knowing that naturally flows when one is connected to Source, or when functioning as an aspect of Oneness.

This was pretty cool, they thought, since now they didn't have to depend on Source or God to tell them what to do. They could make decisions on their own, take charge and forge ahead as they desired. They could experiment and explore in any way they wished without the need to follow God's laws of harmony, balance, respect and love. God was now pretty much out of the picture. They were independent and free to do whatever they wanted, and could now use their creator powers as they wished. This was a really exciting time for those adventurous souls as they learned to rely uniquely on themselves for a change. But what they did not realize is that nothing can ever be separate from Source, or nothing is ever outside of God, so the best they could do was create an illusion, a fantasy, a partial or incomplete expression of Reality.

CHAPTER 6 • FINDING HOPE

Earth was among their later creations and was meant to provide a most extraordinary experience as it held unlimited potential with a never-before-seen range of diversity, from plant to animal and human life. Although the desire to create life on a planet with a physical dimensional focus such as Earth may have been well-intentioned, and in and of itself not wrong, the diminishing awareness of Unity caused by an attempt to function outside of and independently from Source or God would ultimately become untenable.

As the experience of these fundamentally Divine Beings was condensed to lower and lower dimensions, the awareness of their origins faded and their levels of consciousness and awareness diminished tremendously. This is what happened on planet Earth. The experience of the lower dimensions was so dense that it became next to impossible for them to remember that they were sparks of light, energy, vibration, or expressions of Divine Mind. While some may have thrived for many generations on Earth, even with the repeated cycle of birth and death, there was always a deep longing for more.

Now functioning with reduced capabilities and without the wisdom or the knowing that comes from being connected to Source, some of their creations fell out of balance. Ways of holding things together were needed, and so systems and control mechanisms were put into place. This was strange, because in the Garden of Eden, or the Kingdom of Heaven, things always managed to work in harmony, so control mechanisms were never needed. As more difficult challenges arose such as extreme weather conditions, or turbulent galactic energies, they suddenly realized that they did not have the power they believed they had since they could not control these conditions. The adventure into separation—life in denial of God—was beginning to lose some of its charm.

It wasn't long before these adventurous souls began to perceive themselves as disempowered beings, or victims of forces beyond their control. Believing themselves to be disconnected from their safe, balanced, abundant, loving Source, now living in denial of God, fear became their primary driving force, replacing the natural flow of their innate Pure Life Force. In time, the belief that they were small, powerless, individual entities, separate from Source, living in a vast, increasingly frightening universe, facing constant lack and need became the foundation of their existence. What they had essentially created was a made-up world founded on the complete disconnection from Source or God that existed outside of Oneness. In other words, a fantasy world was born, but they were no longer aware that it was a world of their own making.

This deeply-entrenched belief in separation from Source, and ultimately from each other, established a lack of essential integration with the Whole, very much limiting their potential experience and growth. The belief in separation from Source thus established the very foundation for the current experience of life on Earth. Not surprisingly, divisiveness has become like a cancer that has infiltrated all aspects of the human experience, from racial to cultural, religious, gender, medical, educational, political, geographic and economic. In order to heal ourselves of this cancer, we must now open up to the idea that perhaps we are a part of something more, that there is something far greater to be experienced, and with that openness, we can reignite our innate curiosity. Without a correction of this error of separation, without the reintegration of unity consciousness, inclusiveness, oneness, harmony, balance and above all, love, nothing on planet Earth will change substantially.

So the big secret is out. The root of all problems experienced by humanity throughout history, and very likely by other beings in other galaxies, dimensions or planes of existence, is essentially the denial of God, or the disconnection from Source—the greatest breakup of all time. Our primary problem is our acceptance of the belief that it is actually possible to function outside of Oneness, separate from Source, with no actual ties to that Oneness. We prove this to ourselves every minute of every day as we live our lives in a state of incompleteness, or denial of God. This may be what the Bible originally referred to as "the fall" or "original sin." Except that it's not a sin, as humans would deem it, since Pure Life, or God cannot and will not judge, condemn or punish its own creations. It's simply that along the way we—that's us, the adventurous souls—became so caught up in our little creative adventures that we forgot that we are, and always will be, essential elements of the Wholeness of Pure Life.

In so doing, as beings infused with the natural ability to create, we have created the illusion of a world—and very likely many worlds—that appears to function in a state of separation from Source. And that's the core problem; that's what's going on. It is just an error based on the complete absence of the memory of the truth of who and what we are as Divine expressions of Source, or God. As a result, now mostly motivated by fear, we ignore and exclude some of the essential components of Pure Life in expression such as balance, harmony, compassion, inclusiveness, creative intelligence, respect and love. Without these, there can only be fear, lack, competition, disillusionment, suffering, struggle, divisiveness and the absence of true Love. So it is easy to understand how we now find ourselves in a world, a creation of our own making that appears to lack coherence and is in great need of healing.

> In the Creation, God projected His Creative Ability from Himself to the Souls He created, and He also imbued them with the same loving will to create.... No Child of God can lose this ability because it is inherent in what he IS, but he CAN use it inappropriately. (ACIM, Ch. 2, pp. 20-21)

The Solution

The idea that God or some all-powerful force did not put us here in a body, in this human condition, and that it is a result of choices we have made is indeed a lot to take in! There must be a solution for this dire situation, right? How can we fix this separation thing? Fortunately for us, not all expressions of Source, or original Divine Beings bought into the separation narrative. There are those who never went down that rabbit hole and have always remained aware that they are Divine Beings of Pure Light, individual, unique aspects of the great Oneness of Life. And since Creation is always in expression, new beings are likely emerging all the time. Some of these new souls may choose to avoid the path of separation, preferring the experience of Oneness.

Most cultures around the world have carried stories of angel-like beings that reside beyond the Earth realm and watch over life on Earth. Today there are many stories of beings from other galaxies or dimensions who have always maintained that connection to Source. There are also others who did explore separation, but never quite lost the awareness of the truth of their Oneness, such as Jeshua and the Buddha. Knowing from firsthand experience what separation was like put them in an excellent position to help their adventurous brothers and sisters, those of us who had become entangled in the experience of separation.

The solution to this problem of separation is to reclaim our Oneness as integral expressions of Pure Life. While the solution may appear simple, it probably will not be easy—actually, for many, even most, it will be rather challenging. The hardest part is to accept the possibility that this is so. Given our thousands of years of experience in a state of separation and the resulting deeply engrained indoctrination, the term "Oneness" might turn some people off. "Oh no, in Oneness I will cease to exist! I will disappear! I will lose my special traits, those skills I worked so hard at developing. I'll be swallowed up into that great black hole of eternity! Besides, is this even real?"

As a starting point, it can be helpful to remind yourself of what it feels like to be part of something, a group, a family or a community where you do not cease to exist, where you have a special place, where you can simply be yourself. As a member of a group or community, what you do matters because it has an impact on the other members of the group. Plus, you get the added benefit of feeling worthy, like you belong, like others truly care for you. If you have not yet had this experience, it may be worth putting it on your Bucket List, or your wishlist, if only to get a feeling for it. This experience of belonging and feeling worthy will be very well supported in the Aquarius Era.

CHAPTER 6 · FINDING HOPE

Show Me Some Proof!

But, you may wonder, who else in the world is ready for these far-out notions? None of my family or friends are into this stuff. How is this world ever going to change to one of peace, inclusiveness, equality, love and abundance for all when this separation problem is so deeply entrenched, when there has been war, divisiveness, hierarchies, competition for thousands of years? No one I know is aware of this! Just look at what is going on in the world. Divisiveness seems to be spreading like wildfire!

Like many, I had my doubts about this shift that is supposed to be happening on Earth at this time. From where I stood, it didn't look like anything was changing, at least not in my town, which happens to be among the largest cities in North America. I wanted to know that there were others who were looking for answers, others who truly wanted a better world for all, others who were brave enough to do whatever it takes to bring about this shift, but I wasn't seeing it. I wanted proof; I wanted evidence that others were engaging in this quest.

Isn't it said somewhere: "Ask and ye shall receive"? Well, I received an answer to this request while on the bus one day. It was a Saturday afternoon, and I was on the express bus on my way home from a lovely lunch downtown with my daughter and grandson. There were only four of us on the bus: there was a young woman near the front, I was somewhere in the middle, on the right side of the bus, and there were two more people sitting way at the back. After settling into my seat, ready for the 35-minute ride, I noticed that the driver was listening to a lecture or an audiobook on a small device attached to the dashboard. He was a young man, maybe mid- to late-twenties. His slightly tanned skin and facial features led me to think that he was perhaps of Lebanese origin. This was not unusual as there were many from that country residing in Montreal.

Since this was an express bus with only two stops at the end of its route—mine being the very last—this allowed the driver to pick up speed along the way, especially in those stretches when there were no red lights or while on the service road next to the highway. When the bus was in acceleration mode, I couldn't hear much from his device due to the rumbling noise of the engine, but when the bus slowed or came to a stop, words came through surprisingly clearly or, more accurately, surprising words came through clearly!

The lecture or book he was listening to was spoken in English, but there were a few words here and there that I did not understand. They sounded Middle Eastern, maybe Lebanese. It was difficult to understand the words given the normal noise of the bus. Plus, he was behind one of those Plexiglas panels that were installed during the pandemic. But while at the stops, or in those less noisy stretches, I caught several phrases such as "time of change," "finding balance," "creating a new world," and words like consciousness, choice, awareness, mind, love and peace. Now and then the young bus driver would thrust up his right hand and with a clenched fist mumble something, as though he was saying: "Yes! This is what I want!" From where I sat, with only a partial view of his face, I could see the passion, the joy and the excitement in his expression.

I was so surprised by what I was hearing on this rumbling, noisy ride that I didn't know whether I wanted to laugh or cry. Probably both. Fortunately, I managed to hold back the tears. I don't really like to cry in public. I just shook my head in awe. These were topics for which I had been gathering notes over the previous several months. This was my subject of interest, the subject I could not discuss with anyone in my immediate surroundings, other than a couple of friends. And here was this young man, a simple bus driver, listening to a talk on this very subject! It just goes to show that we really have no idea where a person is at—no idea whatsoever, so it is indeed very wise to never judge a book by its cover!

Finally, we reached the terminus. Not in a hurry to get off the bus, I waited for the other passengers to go first. When it was my turn, I couldn't leave without saying something to this brave, young, beautiful soul. But I didn't know what to say. All I wanted was to reach out and connect with him. Finally, I got up, walked to the front, and stood by the glass panel. I smiled as the bus driver looked

CHAPTER 6 • FINDING HOPE

up at me, no doubt accustomed to the "thank yous" and "mercis" he frequently receives from passengers during his shift.

"Thank you," I said, and smiled again. "We are creating a new world." He looked at me inquisitively, a little confused by my comment. He didn't seem to know how to respond. I leaned forward to the right, a bit closer to the edge of the glass that separated us and gave a quick nod toward his audio device, and then I repeated, "Yes, we are creating a new world."

He immediately lit up, with a look of surprise and joy. He smiled and nodded, thoughtfully, as though looking for an appropriate response. He then put his hands together in prayer position in front of his heart and bowed his head in acknowledgment, clearly moved.

"Thank you," I said again, and then stepped off the bus. Feeling so uplifted, feeling my heart so filled with love and light and joy, I smiled all the way home, chuckling and shaking my head with every other breath. I had been wondering if the young people of today were opening up to the possibility that there might be more for humanity on Earth. This brief, but most significant encounter gave me hope. Yes, many are opening up.

And if I needed another little dose of hope, I was given one on the day I was gathering notes for this chapter. It happened while on an afternoon walk with my neighbour, something we do almost every day, just to get some exercise and fresh air. We were walking across the parking lot heading to our favourite grocery store, when all of a sudden I stopped, startled by something I heard a man saying. He was sharing with a friend how he had spent most of his life on a spiritual journey, studying ancient Hindu and other teachings. I couldn't help but look at him and smile. I couldn't hold back, so I said, "Me too!" He looked up at me, startled, but I had to follow my friend in the store. We just smiled. My friend wasn't into this subject at all. If I had been alone, I probably would have joined them in their conversation. But there it was again, proof that we are not alone on this journey, right in the middle of the grocery store parking lot.

And then, as if I needed yet another dose of hope, the evening after I had finished writing this chapter, I attended a concert at the local community centre with a few friends. I wasn't familiar with the band nor was I sure that the music would be my style, but it was an outing with friends, and that's all that mattered. To my great surprise, the event turned out to be so much more! This was a contemporary jazz fusion style band, and they played pieces composed by saxophonist Beth McKenna. It was awesome. For this event, they played the songs from her album titled "Beyond Here." If I needed proof that young people were searching for more, there it was: six amazing young and incredibly talented musicians playing from their hearts, filled with joy. The music carried the themes of letting go, shifting perspectives, leaving behind divisiveness and going towards Oneness, turning away from the noisiness of the world, trusting the Inner Self and the importance of the ripple effect of our actions.

Well, needless to say, I was blown away. I had asked for proof that the world was changing, and there it was again. Plus, I got another little dose of hope that we were moving towards a better world for all life on Earth. I guess there are upsides to living in a big city rather than being tucked away in a monastery.

CHAPTER 7

Home Away from Home

It [the body] takes the central place in every dream, which tells the story of how it was made by other bodies, born into the world outside the body, lives a little while, and dies, to be united in the dust with other bodies dying like itself. (ACIM, Ch. 27, p. 641)

The Times They Are A-Changin'

Indeed, as the Bob Dylan song goes, the times they are definitely changing, and there is no getting around that fact! But, if we want a different experience for ourselves, for mankind, for all life on Earth as well as for our home planet, if we really want something new, not just some patched up, recycled version of the old, then we will need to do things differently. And the great news is that indeed, we are doing things differently, at least we are trying to. Many are learning about our history as a way of better understanding how we got to where we are now. Others are examining how things are being done today in all aspects of life, from home and family to economics, industry and governance, and then exploring how they could be improved. Some are becoming free of the need to hold back by speaking out, or writing, while others are simply showing how to be different through non-judgmental, compassionate, mindful acts of kindness in their everyday interactions.

Many brave souls around the world from all cultures, backgrounds, generations and walks of life are consciously, courageously, intentionally taking the necessary steps to bring about the change we desire and most certainly need. Even if they are only baby steps, no matter how tiny, it is those baby steps that are contributing to the creation of the new world we so deeply desire. These steps, no matter how awkward or clumsy they may seem, should be highly valued, encouraged, nurtured and appreciated since, if they were not taken, nothing would change, no progress would be made and we'd remain stuck with the same old same old.

Okay, so, maybe we want something new, something different, but again, does it have to be so difficult? Things don't seem to be getting any better on Earth; in fact they seem to be getting worse. We have ongoing wars, corruption at all levels of society, increasing divisiveness, growing economic uncertainty, rising poverty, confusion and disagreement on just about every topic, not to mention the mess we are creating on our home planet. How long can this condition be sustained? How bad does it have to get before we do things differently? Is there actually anything we can do? Were the prophesies right? Are we heading for total annihilation? The End Times are upon us!

Whether or not we like it, whether or not we desire it, the transition into the new Era is now underway, and there is no turning back. Given the intensity of this transition, it is having a huge impact on everyone, causing many to reflect, question, re-evaluate and shift their perspectives on the meaning of life. Many are feeling challenged in some, even in all aspects of their lives, from personal to professional. A growing number are ready to consider that there might be more and that there might be a far better way to live life on Earth. Given the intensity of the turmoil and discomfort, this transition has the potential to take humanity to a whole new experience.

As we head into the unknown, more than ever it is vitally important that we become self-aware, that we reach deep inside and begin to uncover the truth of who and what we are. From there, we will know what actions need to be taken, which path is most appropriate for us, what to release as well as what to explore. Fortunately, becoming self-aware is very much in line with the nature of the Era of Aquarius as is evidenced by the fact that it has become a common topic of discussion today. This deep self-awareness will be a key to

CHAPTER 7 • HOME AWAY FROM HOME

our exploration and eventual knowing of the more of who and what we are. There is so much more to be lived and experienced in this vast, infinite universe, so much more to who and what we are, and we live in a time when we are ready to question, explore, and above all experience this for ourselves.

An interesting aspect of the 26,000-year cycle of the Eras, or the Great Year, is that it progresses backwards, that is, from the last, or most complex sign, to the first, or least complex sign. In other words, throughout the Eras we journey around the zodiac from Pisces to Aries. As illustrated in AARCT, it's like going down a ladder, one step, or one Era at a time. At the end of the Era of Aries, approximately 2000 years ago, we leaped to the top of a new ladder into the Era of Pisces. This huge leap marked the start of another journey down the ladder of the Eras. So it is that as we shift from Pisces to Aquarius, we take one step down the ladder.

Several years ago, when I first realized this unique characteristic of the Great Year, I found it to be deeply disturbing. We were going backwards! This system could only lead to ultimate destruction or even annihilation. It was the dreaded Armageddon that had been prophesized for thousands of years. How could we possibly survive this leap? We were heading down the ladder!

Then the dark memory of George Orwell's book *1984* came to mind. That had been a hard-hitting read back in high school, and in fact, it had inspired me to write my best paper ever, with a focus on the subject of freedom. Somehow, over fifty years ago, the child in me knew that one day a great cry for freedom would be expressed by all living beings on Earth. Today, that cry can be heard, loud and clear, right around the world. This cry is entirely natural, even essential, as we transition into Aquarius, the Era that thrives on freedom, independence, and sovereignty. Plus, given the merging of recent technological advancements with the long-standing systems of control, here we are, I thought, living in that dreaded post-Orwellian time. There seemed to be no hope.

However, I eventually came to see this unusual movement in a positive light. It made sense that this trek through the Eras would be a backwards one since it paralleled a movement that was contrary to the natural flow of life, a movement engaged in by adventurous souls who had claimed separation from Pure Life, or Source. It was an attempt to live life in denial of God, an attempt that was futile, since separation from the Infinite is impossible. It was only natural that it would carry at its core a mechanism that would ultimately force us to stop, take a look, and eventually reclaim what had been lost and abandoned. It is like pulling on a stretch band as far as it can go, until you reach the limit of the stretch where you can no longer pull because the resistance is too great. At that point, you must let go and, preferably, gently, steadily allow the band to pull you back to the starting position.

This unique attribute of the cycle of the Eras may explain the apocalyptic nature of ancient prophecies. They were simply forecasts made by individuals who were consciously or perhaps unconsciously in tune with or inspired by the natural cycles and rhythms of creation. It would be like making a dire prophecy on a clear, warm, autumn day where I live in Montreal. "You better get your winter gear ready because in a few weeks, there will be snow and ice on the ground and you will have frostbite and all the plants in your garden will die and your car will slide on ice and veer off into the ditch." I would simply be forecasting upcoming weather trends based on natural cycles of nature.

While I might be right about the loss of the plants in the garden, would I be right about your choices? How could I predict with absolute certainty what would happen to you, since you remain always free to choose what you will or will not do? How would I know what you will do when the temperature drops below freezing? Maybe you already have your winter clothes in the hallway closet ready to wear, including that brand-new pair of ice skates. Maybe you have a set of winter tires by the entrance of the garage. Even if I knew you were an avid skater, I wouldn't know with absolute certainty if you would be skating next winter. Perhaps you decided to do something completely different and you purchased tickets for a winter getaway in Hawaii. No one can predict your experience

CHAPTER 7 • HOME AWAY FROM HOME

because you get to create it with your choices. And even the climate is not absolutely predetermined as it varies from one year or decade or century to another.

So it is with the cycle of the Eras. Plus, as we are now learning, we actually have a far greater role to play in its unfolding than we realize. We are not the powerless, insignificant, unimportant little critters we have for so long believed ourselves to be. While we may have forgotten our origins, we have not extinguished or in any way diminished that original spark of Divine Pure Life. Who and what we are remains available for us now; all that is needed is for us to claim it now. So, instead of wasting time on predictions, forecasts or prophecies, why not focus on the present moment so we can ensure that we are creating the best possible experience for all life on Earth in the new Era. We definitely can go through this transition with grace. There is absolutely nothing that says that it must be an Armageddon or a sixth mass extinction. How we will experience it is entirely up to us.

The increasing resistance and discomfort inherent in the progression through the cycle of the Eras applies to our adventure or experiment into separateness, our fantasy journey away from Source. It was inevitable that we would one day reach a point where the unnatural pull away from our original condition as Divine expressions of Pure Life, Light, Love and infinite potentialities would be so strong that we would have no choice but to stop and pay attention to that uncomfortable tug calling us back to our true nature.

Although mostly unaware of this fact, the adventurous souls who had become lost in the woods and forgotten their way home had an innate guidance system that would eventually lead them back home. This is the tug that many are feeling today. Somehow, just having a good life isn't cutting it anymore. The discomfort, the confusion, the disillusionment, the grief we are experiencing goes far beyond the pain of living in a world of chaos. It is the deep pain of living in a way that is unnatural for beings that are inherently expressions of a balanced, harmonious, loving, Pure Life Source, or Mother/Father/God. It is the natural pull back to our true heritage, the call to gently release the old—the key here being gently—and reclaim the truth of our nature as Divine Beings, as beloved children of God.

The Gift of Life

Again, while these were interesting ideas, even nice metaphors, ones that helped make the journey a bit easier, I was still curious to know more about our incarnations on Earth. Incarnation didn't always seem like a gift; at times, it even seemed more like a curse, or a punishment. We go through birth, the challenges of life, and inevitable death. Why do we keep coming back? Why don't the adventurous souls—we, the children of God—just turn around, leave the forest and go back Home? Why have we no memory of our origins as Divine Beings? Why are we so clueless about the vast expanse and the infinite potentialities of Pure Life in its essential state of balance, harmony, oneness, creativity and love?

For some, the incarnation experience still holds some allure. They enjoy it and want to come back, again and again. Besides, where else would they consider going, since they have forgotten their origins? Others may incarnate as a means of correcting past errors, or to acquire new learning so they may then move on to other, perhaps broader, or higher levels of experience. Some come to Earth to serve and help their brothers and sisters. There are as many reasons for incarnating in the physical realm as there are souls choosing to incarnate. It follows that each soul will choose the family, society, culture and environment that will give them the experience they desire as well as the experience they need for their learning and growth. This is why it is important for each individual to identify for themselves the purpose of their journey so as to make the best of it—to grow, heal, discover, learn and eventually reach up and reclaim the Divine Child that lies in waiting.

Reincarnation has been taught and accepted for aeons in many cultures around the world. However, there are still some people, especially in Western traditions, who do not accept the notion at all. They have one life, and if they are good, if they obey the laws and the rules, they will be allowed into Heaven after they die. In a way, this takes some of the pressure off since they don't need to look beyond their everyday, present life, and less pressure can make the journey seem easier.

There are also many who do not accept the idea that they have chosen their incarnation. A few will go so far as to say that our souls are recycled and sent back to Earth by powerful dark forces that will then use our energies for their benefit. Sounds like quite the sci-fi movie! Others believe that they had no choice but to come back in order to pay for their sins or their bad karma. Some prefer to claim that nobody really knows for sure, so end of discussion; there is no need to ask questions that can't be answered. Any belief a person holds may be helpful if it gives them a sense of peace and the opportunity to learn. Besides, beliefs change over time, especially with first-hand experience. So, flexibility regarding beliefs can be very beneficial as we move forward into a new experience.

The concept of past, let alone parallel lives, may be challenging for some as we step into the Era of Aquarius, as the fixed signs (Aquarius, Taurus, Leo and Scorpio) take great pride in their knowing—or, what they think they know. Many will not accept these unusual ideas until they have valid proof, and the most acceptable proof in the Era of Aquarius will always be first-hand personal experience. Others will wait for science to validate these unusual ideas, and they may be surprised as science, at least non-mainstream science, is making giant leaps in that direction. In the meantime, we can open our minds and consider possibilities, which is also a valid alternative given the inherently curious nature of Aquarius. Maybe, just maybe there is more to be experienced and known.

A good place to explore the idea of previous incarnations is right at home, with family members. For example, when you look at the personality, character traits, unique skills and behaviour of each child born in the same family, you cannot help but wonder why one is musical, while the other is more mechanical; why one is social while the other prefers to stay home and read books. They were raised by the same parents, inherited the same genetics, ate the same foods, went to the same schools, lived in the same neighbourhood and were indoctrinated with the same belief systems yet, very often, they are inherently different. So why is it that, while we may share some family traits, ranging from exceptional talents, skills and abilities, to special interests and preferences, we are fundamentally different from our siblings or even our parents and grandparents?

At the same time, we may also carry within us deeply ingrained fears, traumas and wounds, aspects of ourselves that are in need of healing that may not appear to originate in our current family or cultural heritage. It can only be that we each bring into our life distinct attributes, most likely developed or acquired during past life experiences, perhaps even in other dimensions or on other planets. Maybe you have a fear or something that recurs in your life that is disturbing, but there doesn't seem to be an event in your life that has caused it. This would be a good opportunity to consider that perhaps something in a prior life is the source of the issue. Simply ask yourself, "Where does this come from? What can I learn from this situation or condition?" Once the lesson has been learned, you can then claim: "I'm ready to release this now. I am free of this fear." Then, just let it go.

Our current perception of who and what we are is so limited by our 3-D physical perspective that we really don't know ourselves very well. We certainly do not see ourselves as Divine Beings of love, light and energy. While it is not necessary to dig out all of our past lives, sometimes a little snippet here and there can give us the insight or the "aha" needed to help us recognize, understand, learn, and let go so we can experience the healing and freedom we desire. By releasing the traumas, wounds and burdens of the past, we carry less weight. This is the healing that will clear the way forward so we may discover the more of who and what we are.

One night a few years ago, I had a "flash," or perhaps it was a "vision," I'm not sure what to call it. Sometimes I can't find the right words to describe some of these experiences. Anyhow, I saw myself standing outside, in what appeared to be a nonphysical dimension,

CHAPTER 7 • HOME AWAY FROM HOME

beyond the world as we know it. There I stood, facing the prospect of incarnating on Earth. I had a sense that I was standing tall and firm in my position as I said, "Okay, I'll go back one more time." The words and the intention were clear and firm, but there was also a hint of impatience, perhaps even resentment or annoyance. I wasn't sure at the time what exactly I was feeling about the idea of reincarnating. However, that brief experience certainly provided hints of powerful learning opportunities that were yet to come.

Many are claiming that they will definitely not be returning to Earth. This is often expressed with a certain disdain or contempt, as though the human experience is something beneath them, something despicable. "This is my last incarnation on Earth! I am ascending!" they boldly declare. And I feel for them. I understand perfectly where they are coming from, as I swore the same thing not so long ago. It's easy to take that position, especially as we are learning that the truth about who and what we are has been kept hidden from the general population for thousands and thousands of years. Basically, we've been lied to. Plus, who wants to return to a world filled with increasing control measures, inequality, greed, fear, corruption, poverty, never-ending war, and the list goes on! This would seem like a natural, logical response to the question of whether or not one should reincarnate on Earth. "There must be better places out there somewhere, right? Where's that Heaven they keep talking about? I want to go there!"

However, is this response our highest expression possible? Does it reveal the most enlightened view of what is occurring here on Earth? Is it filled with understanding, kindness, love and compassion? But above all else, is it a perspective that Pure Life, or Mother/Father/God, our loving Creator, would hold? With a condescending, or demeaning attitude towards life on Earth, or towards any aspect of Creation, perhaps there is some baggage being carried forward from the past, clouding the vision of what is and what might be. An Earth experience may stir up memories of past indiscretions, errors, poor choices that carry deep guilt, shame, or fear of punishment. This kind of response may simply be a reaction to a dark history. It can then be turned into an excellent opportunity to clear the way for a more divine experience through the practice of forgiveness. Ultimately, no matter how dark, the past must be forgiven so that it can be released, freeing us to move forward.

While working on this chapter, I decided to take a break, go out for a walk and enjoy the sunshine. Winter was coming to an end. A flock of geese had already flown overhead towards their favourite spot by the river indicating that spring was just around the corner. As I arrived at the parking lot across from the grocery store I frequently go to, I paused and looked up at the sky. There were my favourite feathered friends. I love watching the pigeons dance across the sky, how they always fly in harmony, shining like little diamonds as the sun's rays light them up. What is captivating is how their colours vary so widely from pink to green, blue, white and black, making each one unique. Yet, despite the fact that they are all different from each other, they manage to fly together, never crashing into each other, never competing or fighting. They simply flow in the sky in beautiful perfect harmony.

This time, I saw a woman emptying a bag of birdseed at the base of a tree where the pigeons gather daily to eat whatever people leave for them. We smiled at each other, recognizing our mutual love of these little creatures, and ended up having a lively, friendly chat. We both agreed on how beautiful they are, how amazing it is to watch them fly together in harmony, with the words God and love thrown into the conversation. It was sweet. But then she concluded by mentioning how horrible humans are in comparison to these beautiful birds. Again, this is something I have heard many times. I have even seen social media posts expressing that humans are so horrible that they deserve to be completely removed from Earth. But is that all there is to our story? We are horrible creatures and should be punished, even annihilated for our horribleness?

Why is that? Why is it so difficult for us to see beyond, to see God, our Creator, the Divinity in each and every person regardless of what they are doing? Why is it that we are not seeing Pure Life everywhere we look if Pure Life is the Source of All That Is? Until

CHAPTER 7 • HOME AWAY FROM HOME

we have returned to that heart-centred place, until we know true Love, the Love of Pure Life, the Love of the Creator, most likely there are some lessons that need to be learned. What better school than embodiment on Earth, bound by the limitations of the 3-D physical experience, sharing a journey with billions of our brothers and sisters. This is indeed a school filled with tremendous, invaluable learning opportunities!

There were times when I felt resentful about living in this huge, noisy, busy city of over 4 million people, wishing that I could move to a small town, with a simple, quiet, harmonious community lifestyle. This huge city is very diverse, but it could use a little more community spirit. We have a provincial government that is constantly pushing the French versus English narrative, amplifying divisiveness instead of unity and community. So, I must admit that I was a bit jealous of those who lived the simple life out in the country, with like-minded souls, surrounded by nature instead of divisiveness, noise and pollution. Then one day, while out for a walk, pondering this very question, the answer came: "You are surrounded by over 4 million souls in need of love. What more could you ask for!" "Oh my, yes!" I replied as my heart swelled with that most glorious feeling, that feeling that pushes tears right up to your eyes when Truth emerges. Indeed, with over 4 million opportunities to love, what more could one ask for!

While some believe that they have no choice and the cycle of birth, life and death is out of their control, my understanding is that, ultimately the soul does not need to incarnate in a body. However, for the Divine Self, or the child of God who has forgotten what it is because of repeated incarnations in a state of separation, being in a body may be the quickest—or perhaps even the only—way to re-know the truth of who and what we are. There comes a point where the confinement and limitation of the physical experience becomes unbearable. At that point, our perception of the body should simply be recognized for what it is: a momentary distraction acting as a boundary keeping us from the full experience of who and what we are as Beings originating from a Source of infinite potentialities,

Beings of Life, Love and Light. Perhaps another way to see it is as a wake-up call. Rather than being demeaned, condemned or feared, the experience of human incarnation can be seen as a great opportunity that inevitably clears the way to what lies beyond ancient, long-held beliefs. It invites us to be curious to know if that's all there is, and be open to the more that can be experienced.

At first, some of the elements we carry forward into our lives from past incarnations may be perceived as heavy burdens, or even as forms of punishment. But, as our perspective broadens and our understanding of who and what we are expands, all that is encountered can be re-known and turned into powerful learning opportunities. Never underestimate the healing power of something that calls your attention, something that causes you to take a closer look inside, since what is inside is carried forward until it has been released. Plus, you can only release what you see, what has been acknowledged and recognized so, again, look inside; you may discover a goldmine of wisdom and knowledge in that great gift of Pure Life. Besides, Life is a far greater teacher than what is found in books since Life needs to be lived and firsthand experience is where true knowing emerges.

The following Daily Message from Jeshua came just at the right time, on the right day. Thank you!

> You have chosen, as the god that you are, as the angel that you are, as the Light energy, the consciousness of Light energy, you have chosen to know what it feels like to be amongst your creations; not only to be amongst them, but to activate them and to see what it feels like. (Jeshua Online—Daily Message)

While inserting the above quote into this chapter, tears flowed as the final movement of Rachmaninoff's Piano Concerto No. 2 filled the energy of my space. This time, I had decided to listen to all four concertos. Thank goodness for the dusty old CD player! Yes, the Light energy is with us. This piece of music takes me right there, overcoming any doubts or obstacles that might stand in the way. Okay, time for Piano Concerto No. 3. Note that, while I am still not quite sure why I have had these "musical therapy" experiences, I wouldn't change them for anything in the world! I also know that not everyone will resonate with the same music or with any music at all, and that's okay. What is important is to look for what stirs the angel, the child of God, the divine soul that lies within so you may awaken to your True Self.

Born Free

Born free? Well, that may be true for wild tigers and giraffes and reindeers and butterflies, but that's not quite true for us humans. Nor do we just land here on Earth on a gust of wind ready for adventure, free to live and explore life—at least not at this time. So, let's go back to a beginning that is a bit closer to home, the start of our present life, or, the process of incarnation. Note that the following is simply a story made up for the purpose of providing a different perspective on the subject.

If you think about it, the way a being, a soul, or a spark of life takes on physical form in order to experience life on Earth is quite interesting. The original entry point for the soul moving into this level of incarnation is very specific, as it requires the joining of a sperm, provided by a soul in a male body, and an egg, provided by a soul in a female body. At least that's the natural way it works. In this early stage of preparation for incarnation, the masculine and feminine energies work together in perfect harmony in order to create a form, or a vehicle, for the soul's journey, all within a safe, nurturing receptacle, or womb. This harmonious collaboration between the masculine and feminine is a reflection of the natural process of creation as is expressed by Pure Life.

First, the sperm must find its way out of the male body and then be introduced into the female body. In order to ensure that sufficient wombs were created to meet the demand for human incarnation, a sensory pleasure was attached to the interaction. This extraordinary experience shared by two souls was originally intended to be a gentle joining, a natural, loving sharing of momentary Oneness. It was an intimate experience of the nature of Pure Life, where subtle, gentle, yet powerful energies merged harmoniously to prepare a portal for a new soul desiring to experience life through incarnation on Earth.

Over time, as awareness of their divine origins as expressions of Pure Life, Love and Light faded from memory, humans focused more on the physical, sensory aspect of their experience of incarnation. The strong sensory component of the joining of bodies further strengthened and very likely contributed to limiting and locking in awareness to the physical aspect of incarnation. As identification with the physical body gained supremacy for those incarnated in human form, the act of intercourse was increasingly misused. The process of preparing the womb then became very energetic, sometimes even aggressive or violent. Due to its extremely intense nature, this interaction between two beings now tends to overshadow any experience that lies beyond the physical dimension, standing instead as the ultimate human experience.

What was originally meant to be an expression of the pure, balanced, nurturing energies of Creation was eventually reduced to a purely physical interaction. As the act was misused, shame and guilt were attributed to it, and rules as to how and when to engage in it were established. But the question remains, was it really shame and guilt over the act of two bodies coming together that was the problem? Or was there something else driving that shame and guilt, something far deeper? If there is a forgetting of our true origins, might the remembrance of our origins as Divine expressions of Source simply clear away the shame, the guilt and the misuse of what was originally meant to be a harmonious, natural act of creation?

Although humans refer to this act of preparing a womb for a soul's incarnation as "making love," which was no doubt true in the early stages of human incarnated life, today the fact is that love may have little or even nothing to do with it. As humans settled into the physical experience, forgetting completely about the energy of their Divine origins, this act was for the most part reduced to a response to a call for gratification of a sensory urge. That is what drives the

CHAPTER 7 · HOME AWAY FROM HOME

physical desire; it is not necessarily driven by love. While there may be a certain amount of love, even an overwhelmingly heart-warming sense of caring and love exchanged between two beings who wish to share in this pleasurable act, love is not a requirement.

On the other hand, this act is not a requirement for the expression of love, as love expresses far beyond the physical dimension. If it were truly driven by love—true Love—the act of intercourse would not be misused or abused in any way. In fact, it could not be misused since true Love, which is an expression of Pure Life, functions on a foundation of the principles of balance, harmony and, above all, honour and respect for all Creation. Of itself, there is nothing inherently wrong with intercourse; it is not evil or bad. It is simply an opportunity for two souls who care for each other to experience unity and to share love through a pleasurable physical exchange. What matters is the purpose for which it is engaged in. It is indeed a wonderful way for two souls to have an experience of the oneness everyone seeks, the unique joining that provides that sense of true wholeness.

Okay, so now that the conjoined sperm and egg have settled in the uterus and transformed into an embryo, it will continue to grow until it is ready to welcome a new soul into the world. The adventurous soul that takes residence in this womb will have chosen it for its eventual learning and experiential opportunities. Meanwhile, during those months spent in the womb growing and developing the necessary organs and systems for human incarnation, the soul will be surrounded by safe, warm, caring, welcoming energies. It will experience the natural abundance, safety, love, balance, harmony and nurturing that is inherent in Pure Life, Source or God. It is like a brief moment in time when the truth of its Oneness with Source is experienced first-hand, when the Soul knows what it is like to truly be Home, where there is no fear, no lack, no threat or danger of any kind. That seed of Oneness will remain always within the soul as it journeys through its incarnations on Earth, since it carries the truth of its original conception as a Divine expression of Source, and truth can never be taken away.

As the incarnating soul develops its body in readiness to experience life on Earth, it grows in excitement. Since it has long forgotten its origins, like the adventurous souls who wandered off in the forest it looks forward to the possibility of finding its way home in this new incarnation. "This is going to be fun! I'll get to develop my special skills again, maybe even become an expert in that field I find so fascinating. Maybe this time around, I can also heal some of those ancient wounds and while I'm at it, I can get rid of that old garbage I don't want to carry around anymore. Then I can learn a bunch of new things. And I so look forward to meeting some of my old friends! Can't wait to incarnate again!"

Welcome Home

Then comes the exciting part. "Quick! She's going into labour; she's having contractions! The baby is coming!"

"Oh no!" the tiny, incarnating soul cries. "What's happening to my warm, safe, comfortable home? It's a womb quake! It's the end of the world! I'm being pushed out of my nest! Ouch! This must be Armageddon!"

And the birthing process is officially underway. In time, whether minutes or hours, the adventurous soul finally emerges from its rough ride through that dark, tight tunnel. While it is true that some souls may at this point change their minds about incarnating and simply leave the foetus, most will be brave enough to endure the process so they can continue with their adventure into human incarnation. A whole life lies ahead! There is much to be excited about.

"Whoa! What was that," the soul cries as it gasps that first breath of harsh, dry air. "Where am I? Or more importantly, who am I?" That intense ride through the tunnel seems to have blurred any awareness of the purpose or intention of this journey, and it now has no idea of where it is or where it is going. "I want to go back home!" it cries as loudly as it can. "I want to go back home!" Very soon, it finds itself wrapped in a new womb, a thing made of a dry substance it has not known before, with a pair of long, fleshy things holding it up against a warm mass.

CHAPTER 7 · HOME AWAY FROM HOME

As the mother gently wraps the blanket around her newborn child and draws it close to her heart, she sheds tears of joy, love and relief. "Welcome home my sweet baby Charlie!" The mother places a soft, gentle kiss on the infant's forehead. "Isn't he beautiful?"

"What was that?" I never heard such sounds when I was at home. "What is holding me?"

Soon, the newly incarnating soul settles down. "Hmmm, maybe this isn't so bad after all. Maybe I'll be okay here." It blinks several times as it tries to get a sense of its new home. "But, what's with all those bright lights? I can't see anything. I'll just close my eyes." Feeling somewhat comforted and hoping that this is nothing more than a dream, the newly incarnated soul relaxes and lets itself fall asleep. "When I wake up, I'll be home again in my nice, cozy, warm womb." But, when it wakes up, it immediately realizes that there is no going back; this is its new home. What it does not realize is that this is a home away from that previous home that was actually a home away from its true Home.

And so another adventure into human form has begun. The shift from being in a self-contained, nurturing, warm, safe womb to being out in a space without boundaries, without limitations, surrounded by countless unfamiliar things and strange, large beings is a big one. It is so radical that the newborn soul pretty much forgets anything that was known before that moment of incarnation. Besides having long forgotten its true origins as a Divine expression of Pure Life or, as a child of God, while preoccupied with settling into a new life on Earth it also forgets why it came. More importantly, it forgets that it actually chose to come to Earth. Any plans it held for this new incarnation have faded from memory as it now needs to focus on how to navigate this strange, unfamiliar territory. Survival now becomes a priority. The physical aspect of life on Earth seems to require lots of attention—lots! It has needs which it did not have while in the womb. This is going to require a lot of work!

The experience of separation through the birthing process can be likened to the experience of the adventurous souls who decided to venture out and leave the safety and abundance of their original

Home to create a world of their own making. Once we have left the safety of oneness in the womb and made our appearance in the world, we learn to live in separation, to function, thrive and survive as separate entities. Imagine a young toddler or infant abandoned at the edge of town, all alone, without a parent to care for his needs. Desperate to amend that separation, driven by a deep feeling of loss and a fear of death, that child will accept the first person that comes along and offers help. He will accept their beliefs, teachings, rules, laws and conditions, and he will say yes to whatever is required just to survive the separation.

It is the very nature of the parents of the newborn soul to do their best to provide safety, nurturing, and shelter. However, believing the child to be a blank slate, they most likely have no idea that the child comes into this world with an agenda of their own. Wanting the best for their child, they may impose structures and beliefs that are not in alignment with them. It is no wonder that throughout history, many young souls have felt misunderstood, even unsupported on their journey. At the same time, many parents did not understand where they went wrong when the child stirred in a direction they could not comprehend.

That is how the child in you feels: a deep feeling of loss of connection with its Source, Pure Life, Mother/Father/God, and a sense that it is living far away from its true Home. That is what the child in you does: it looks to mend that broken connection by joining with something, someone, some beliefs outside of himself or herself. This experience of separation through physical embodiment can be repeated, over and over again, but ultimately, it cannot be ignored.

As the seed of Unity with Pure Life, God, or Source has never been removed, one day the adventurous soul asks, "Is there more? Is that all there is?" Until that moment, the newborn soul settles into its experience in a new life. That is the starting point of the human experience on the 3-D level. That is the starting point for each and every single being on Earth at this time. We—each and every one of us—start on a foundation of separation that strengthens the original adventure into separation from Pure Life. Each and every soul then sets out to mend that pain of separation.

Try including this point in your perspective the next time you encounter someone who seems to be struggling, or behaving in a less than gracious manner. This may give you the opportunity to open your heart rather than resorting to what may seem justifiable judgment or criticism. This is what the world needs now—for us to open our hearts.

> The still small voice says, "Come Home and remember who you are, for indeed you are eternity. You are much more than the activity that you see in each day." This allows you to bring forth the joy of the holy Child, to express the Love and the joy in complete freedom. (Jeshua Online—Daily Messages)

The Light Has Come

Do not be afraid
For the light has come
It will hold you up
Comfort you
Guide you
Encourage you
And ultimately, it will heal you.
The light will shine away all darkness
And then you will know
There is nothing to fear.

Michael J. Miller

CHAPTER 8

Reunification

> Many stand guard over their ideas because they want to protect their thought systems as they are, and learning means change. Change is always fearful to the separated ones, because they cannot conceive of it as a change towards HEALING the separation. They ALWAYS perceive it as a change towards further separation, because the separation was their first experience of change. (ACIM, Ch. 4. p. 66)

Re-examining Beliefs

Beliefs have always played a significant role in the foundation and sustaining of our apparent reality. They can be helpful for the adventurous soul navigating their way through another incarnation on Earth, and perhaps in other dimensions as well. "I believe if I turn right on this road I will find my way home; that's what my mom told me, and she's usually right!" They also establish the boundaries that determine which information we will let in or accept, and which information we will outright reject. "We've experienced life in other dimensions? On other timelines? Really? Impossible! I'll wait for science to prove it."

New ideas and teachings can sometimes challenge our boundaries, at least in the beginning, so it is best to go as slowly and as comfortably as possible when exploring new perspectives, especially those that might seem too radical. In this time of great change, there is no denying the abundance—perhaps even overabundance—of new, even seemingly crazy, ideas. An idea that challenges the boundaries too quickly or too radically may cause us to reinforce and strengthen our old, familiar boundaries, to buckle down, and pull back to a more limited way of seeing, thus delaying the move to a higher state of consciousness. "I'm shutting the door. I'm sticking with what I know." What may help ease the shift is the fact that there is no need to worry about new knowledge as it will come when we are ready to accept it, and above all experience it.

It's funny how we don't really examine or question our beliefs; we just hold on to them. It's what we know; it's what we were taught. We don't even need to think about it. For example, on Sunday, you may casually recite that God created us in his image and likeness—at least that's what it says in the Holy Scriptures. Then on Wednesday, while on your way to that biology test, you may be getting ready to explain how we have evolved from apes, as the science of the day teaches. If you think about it, this would mean that God must be some kind of giant ape up in Heaven. If he first created Adam and Eve in his image and likeness—our original ancestors—then they too must have been apes. And if they were apes, how could they be sinners? What most people don't realize is that most ancient teachings are metaphorical or symbolic in nature and were not meant to be taken literally. It was only natural that the distracted, innocent, adventurous souls playing in the forest didn't quite get their true meanings, and so they passed on the teachings in the best way they could.

It's okay and perhaps even very healthy to let some of these beliefs go and explore other possibilities. For example, if you have been trained to believe that the saviour is coming to save you and throughout your life you haven't seen evidence of this, you still have not been saved, perhaps it may be a good idea to explore beyond this belief. What does it mean to be saved? And, saved from what? Perhaps you have been saved, if your saviour is a loving soul, but you just haven't experienced it yet. If you have adopted the view that the world is simply an accident or a mechanical or energetic Big Bang and you feel discomfort, sadness, or lack in your life, how could this accident or Big Bang bring you such misery if it is just a

CHAPTER 8 · REUNIFICATION

neutral, non-judgmental, mechanical event? Perhaps you have been considering some of the new claims that this world is nothing more than a matrix or an illusion yet, how can that be because in your experience, in your life, *you* are most certainly very real. Again, question your line of thought, or your belief. Does it work for you? If not, perhaps it is time to re-evaluate these beliefs and open up to something new, something different.

Many are now questioning the human condition. Who are we? What are we? Why are we here? Who put us here? Is there anything else? These are all difficult questions to ask because as far as we know, we don't seem to have the answers. But the climate of Aquarius allows for questioning—even encourages it—so it is not surprising that these questions are being put forth. And since Aquarius is logical and practical, we should expect answers to these questions that make sense, answers that are straightforward. This is how things grow, evolve, change, and transform. Is there something else? Is there another way? Is there a better way? Out of this innate curiosity, inventions are born, innovation emerges, and a new world is created. But, in the energies of the new Era, information, insights, teachings will need to be practical and logical, rather than symbolic, metaphorical or abstract. This is why it will be important for each one to seek the experience, and not rely on theology.

As we move forward and begin to explore an entirely new consciousness for humanity—a new way of being and knowing—it may be helpful to examine our long-held beliefs. Before anything new can be explored or even considered, some of these may need to be changed, updated, modified or even abandoned. In a way, our beliefs can at times act as crutches, allowing us to function with a certain sense of security. As we shift into a completely new way of being, something that has not been experienced by humanity since the beginning of the experience of separation—basically, as we are now facing the unknown—we will need to adjust our beliefs and adapt them as our needs, understanding and perspectives change. Since we are moving forward very rapidly at this time, it can be uncomfortable to release long-held beliefs, to try new ones and then release them just as quickly. However, this will be necessary as we transition into a new experience for humanity. If we cling to beliefs that are contrary to this shift, we will slow down or delay our unfolding.

One truth, one God, one religion, one culture, one language, one system, one chosen people—this mindset of absolutism extends beyond spiritual, religious or cultural beliefs into science, government and politics. This is a mindset with which I was very familiar throughout my life, having begun my journey with the "one and only church," the Catholic Church. When I set out to explore other teachings, each one became the new "one and only," until I came across the next one. There was even a bit of guilt attached as I left behind one system of thought for another, that's how strong the idea of "one and only" was. Yet, I continued on my quest until I found what made sense to me, what could be a true "one and only," the idea and subsequent experience of Pure Life, that balanced, harmonious, infinite, inclusive, loving Source of all life. With this new language and perspective, I could now recognize and appreciate truth in many ancient and contemporary teachings.

While it can feel comfortable to stand by the "one truth," this mindset is contrary to the diversity of life on planet Earth and in the universe. It is also contrary to the natural Oneness of all creation. How can there be many absolute truths that are also contrary? How can there be many "one and only" gods? They must simply be various ways of seeing things, various ways of experiencing life, but all are included in the same Oneness of Creation. If there is one Source of all Creation, and it expresses itself in infinite ways, there cannot be one of these ways that is the only way, or that is better than any other way. If there were many sources in competition with each other for supremacy, and if these sources were so powerful, would they not have destroyed each other's creations? What kind of Source/God, would that be? It would not be a Source/God founded on or infused with Oneness or the basic principles of Pure Life.

We were taught that we are the product of the joining of a sperm and an egg, we were born, we age and then we die. That is a common belief, and it is not likely to be questioned, and what we dare not question becomes absolute. But is it the whole truth of who and what we are? Is it helpful for our growth, for expanding our self-awareness and for our healing? Are traditional belief systems the only way of gathering information that will help us move forward to a new way of Being? Will they help us during times of challenge and change? We are not likely to question our beliefs when we cling to an absolutist way of thinking.

As Aquarius likes to know, or at least it likes to think it knows, giving up this position may not be easy. By blindly holding onto the past, to what we think we know, we may be limiting our potential experience of Pure Life. Beliefs make life simple. We don't need to question. We just accept, believe and focus on going about our daily lives. They keep us from needing to seek for knowledge deep within, which means that we do not need to rely on ourselves. If we make a mistake, if something goes wrong, it's on "them"—the ones we placed our faith in. It is a way of denying self-empowerment. However, in an Era where sovereignty is an important factor, this kind of faith will not be sustained for very long.

Okay then, let's get real. What if we had it all wrong? What if we are not just insignificant little beings that appear on Earth after the joining of a sperm and an egg, beings that live for a short or long amount of time and then die? What if Mother/Father/God or the Source of Life wasn't out there somewhere, but rather everywhere? Pure Life must be everywhere since It is the Source of all Life in expression. And so Pure Life must be in all things, as well as in all beings, regardless of who and what they believe themselves to be. What if it were true that we have forgotten who and what we are? This belief in separation, which is basically a denial of God, along with the resulting denial of our inherent divinity, will need to be looked at more closely. By maintaining this belief, we effectively turn away from the Source of our Life, the Source of who and what we are, the Source of our infinite creative potential. Without a shift or correction of our beliefs, how will we reclaim the truth of who and what we are as Divine Creator Beings?

Beliefs do not need to be rigid or binding. If they make you feel better, they can be used temporarily as you progress and move forward with your experiences. But then be ready to abandon them as you move forward. The same would apply to teachings. While a teaching may provide fascinating information, inspiration, flashes of understanding, support and encouragement, it does not mean that it will continue to be helpful or even needed forever. Ultimately, it is first-hand experience that will give you the knowledge you need, at which point, those beliefs or teachings that no longer serve or suit your journey may simply be set aside.

Exploring various teachings can be helpful, as each teaching uses its own unique language, imagery and symbolism. This can help release a limiting boundary of understanding, especially as we tend to cling to what we think we know to feel safe or even worthy. Such was my experience when I opened up to other teachings after my deep dive into *A Course in Miracles*, my "one and only" teaching at the time. The varied language found in these teachings, plus my own experience with language and metaphors made the Course, and other works, so much easier to understand. While perhaps using different vocabularies, true teachings will be found to contain the same or similar messages, since the Truth can be expressed in infinite ways. I was then able to fully appreciate these works we are being given at this challenging time of change and transition, when new, more appropriate teachings are very much appreciated. The Truth is true, no matter the language or wording, and it does not need to rely on beliefs. The Truth is simply known, and it remains always accessible for those who seek it.

"*There is another way of looking at the world.*" (ACIM, Lesson 33)

Back to Earth

As Pure Life is infinite and as its natural impulse is to expand, grow, share, and express itself, to be curious, discover, learn and know everything that can be known, so it is that as expressions of Pure Life we must carry the same attributes. We are naturally curious, we enjoy expressing ourselves and sharing our journeys, and we have an innate desire to experience, discover, learn and know everything we can about ourselves, about each other, about the world, and about life. So it is that we come back to Earth, once again.

As we saw, there are many reasons why a soul would choose to incarnate on Earth—from healing past traumas, attending to unfinished business, picking up where they left off, to expanding through new learning and experience, or perhaps even to help and support their fellow adventurous souls. Incarnation in human form is one of the many ways we can use to fulfill these desires. As each soul's journey is unique, it is important for each one to identify the purpose, needs and goals of their present incarnation. In so doing, each one will make the best possible choices for herself/himself as well as the best contribution to the creation of a new world.

Each time we return to Earth, we become more and more proficient at living on this level of manifestation, which in turn provides more knowledge and greater learning opportunities, as well as more ways of expressing our innate creator energies. After countless incarnations, we have effectively become very good at experiencing life in human form. In fact, if we look back at our accomplishments over the past couple of centuries, especially in the fields of technology, industry, commerce and science, we can see that we have effectively become experts at surviving, living and thriving in the physical realm.

However, while we have become quite familiar, and very likely comfortable with incarnation in a body on Earth, it does not mean that we cannot also have access to other levels of experience, such as in other dimensions or on other timelines. We are, after all, expressions of Pure Life and we carry infinite possibilities within us. Yet, we do not seem to experience anything beyond the physical Earth realm. We keep reincarnating, over and over again but, have we found what our heart has been searching for since the start of our journey as separate, independent, adventurous souls? Have we reached our true Home? In fact, we are for the most part not even aware of our deep, inner desire—the desire to return to the more of who and what we are and to reconnect with our true origins as Divine Beings of Love and Light. Why is that?

The choice to incarnate on Earth is not bad, or wrong. The problem lies in the fact that we keep coming back with one important component missing: the awareness of our essential unity with all of Creation, our Oneness with the Source of all Life. While experiencing life from the physical earthly dimension alone, there is very little awareness of anything that may exist beyond it. We are born, we live, we age, and we die. That's life as we know it. We live as though it were possible to be separate from Source, which is contrary to the all-inclusive, loving, nurturing, supportive nature of Pure Life. Even those who claim to believe in God are living in separation, since they put God "out there" somewhere in some far distant heaven, while they struggle or perhaps thrive down here on Earth.

It was thus inevitable that we would find ourselves standing on a foundation of fear—fear of lack, fear for our lives and fear of the unknown that lies beyond our limited perception of reality. This fear was reinforced by the fact that what is physical or material appears to have a limited lifespan. Not only do living forms age, wither and die, but all material things break down, even rocks decompose. Over time, most, if not all of our creations become obsolete, at which point they are no longer needed and are sent to the dumpster. We appear to live in a finite world where everything will ultimately meet its end. And so it is that fear feeds most, if not all, Earth-based beliefs, choices, decisions, and actions. However, fear serves only to sustain the small self or the adventurous soul on its journey into separation, a journey that must come to an end since it is based on an illusion—the illusion of separation from Source. As the Guides channelled through Paul Selig repeatedly remind us: "The purpose of fear is to claim more fear."

Believing ourselves to be separate from our Source and living on a foundation of fear, it was only natural that survival would become our priority. As adventurous souls seemingly lost in a world of our own making, basically living the impossible, our primary focus became the protection of our very existence. While we ignored the

CHAPTER 8 · REUNIFICATION

Oneness of all life in expression, attention to or even interest in anything more than or beyond our physical experience was greatly diminished, and for most, completely obliterated.

Having effectively forgotten who and what we are, we go about our lives with no recollection of our origins as Divine expressions of Pure Life. The desire to know our true Home has taken a turn. Instead, we look for fulfillment in the world of our creation—our familiar environment—where true fulfillment cannot be found. Now completely caught up in the physical aspect of the experience, we focus mainly on attending to basic survival needs. This is understandable since most, if not all, of the structures of the world as we know it are designed for survival. "My dad said that if I get a job in that company, I'll be set for life!" the adventurous soul claims. "When I find the right life partner, I will be happy!" "When I get my own apartment, I'll be free to do as I please." "I must keep that job so I can feed my family." "I need to get that degree so I can have that career that pays well." In our now very familiar environment in human incarnation, unaware of anything that lies within or beyond, we set out to find what we want and get what we need in the world outside of and around us.

In the 3-D experience of separation, we identify primarily as a body, which then acts as a boundary between self and non-self. This separation is mirrored out into the world in countless forms of divisiveness. However, our separateness is so far from our full potential as integral parts of the Oneness of Creation that it cannot be sustained forever. As Aquarius carries the energy of community, many are feeling a call for reunification. For those who desire to go further and reconnect with their true origins, the challenges of this very dense, physical reality can provide great learning and healing opportunities, and may even accelerate the process of reknowing our true potential. That feeling of being constrained or in some way limited or even imprisoned, indicates that something beyond the physical is requiring our attention. In an Era where feeling and freedom will override rules and dogma, it is understandable that many will be searching for that something that lies beyond the known, ready to give it the attention it desires.

Indeed, there is a still, small voice inside—the voice of the child of God that calls out to us. "Hold on, that's not all there is. Come, look inside. You are so much more!" That inner child, the Christ Child, is the spark of the Divine that resides always within us, and while it may have been forgotten while we were busy tending to the physical aspects of our incarnations, it can never be destroyed or taken from us. All expressions of Pure Life remain always whole, complete and at Home, perfectly safe, nurtured and forever loved. This cannot be otherwise as this is the nature of God, and Mother/Father/God could not withhold any of itself from its Creations. And as Mozart's Requiem plays on the radio in the background while I work on this section, I can't help but imagine this exquisite piece of music with new lyrics for a new Era, expressing the Truth of who and what we are. "Come," the Christ Child in you calls out. "Look inside! You will know that you are safe and you are loved. You will know that there is no need for fear. You will know yourself as God created you!"

However, this is not quite what we have been taught, and this is a key point that needs to be addressed during this time of transition. For thousands of years, we have been taught to abide by the belief systems, teachings, laws, rules and regulations in place in the cultures of our chosen incarnations—cultures founded on the belief that it is possible to function independently from Source. We have been taught to listen to those "who know" and to obey the dictates of those who rule and govern, and if you don't abide by the rules, you will be punished. And just to ramp up the drama a little bit, if you are not punished during your life, you're sure as hell going to be punished after you die. While sustainable in the Era of Pisces, fortunately, this fear-inducing emotional drama will not be sustained in the Era of Aquarius.

So why all these rules and regulations? Once functioning as though separate from Source, no longer benefiting from the essential harmonious, respectful, balanced, safe, loving nature of Pure

CHAPTER 8 · REUNIFICATION

Life, the adventurous souls needed to develop rules otherwise chaos would have ensued. So it is that rules and regulations were put into place, and systems were developed and established to meet the various needs of the times. While many of these systems were helpful, unfortunately, motivated by fear as well as a desire to exercise control, some more eager souls began to misuse these systems and regulations, taking positions of dominance, rulership and control over others. However, living in separation and no longer respecting the natural laws of Pure Life, what these souls were experiencing was a false sense of power.

On the other hand, those who were not interested in taking on positions of power simply allowed themselves to be controlled. This was not hard to do because as adventurous souls seemingly living in denial of God, they already felt disempowered. But this sense of powerlessness was just as false as the sense of power the rulers felt. The true power of a child of God cannot be taken away, but it can be ignored. Note that because of the essential law of balance in Creation, one cannot exist without the other. There cannot be a victim without a victimizer, nor a victimizer without a victim. Each adventurous soul chooses to play their role. It is like a dance; you can't have one without the other.

As curious, adventurous souls, we have played various roles throughout our many incarnations. While in some incarnations we may have contributed to the creation and maintenance of these rules, regulations and structures because we chose to play roles of governance and rulership, in other, more laid-back incarnations we simply followed along, doing as we were told. Since we choose our incarnations for the experiences they will provide, we also agree with the structures in place at the time and in the location of our incarnations. This idea may at first be a bit difficult, or even impossible for some to accept, but it does imply that we have one very important gift: the freedom of choice, a very empowering freedom that will require serious consideration. We remain always free to say "no" to a dance that diminishes our essential divinity.

As we saw, it was only natural for the newly incarnated soul to adopt a non-self-reliant approach to life, as it is completely dependent on others for its survival from the moment it takes that very first breath. Interestingly, many parents today are quite taken aback by the sovereign and outspoken nature of their young ones. It appears that those adventurous souls choosing to incarnate today are arriving on Earth with a slightly greater awareness of who and what they are. We can see this in the growing number of children who express unusually advanced skills very early in life, especially in the arts or creative domains. Some are even arriving with clear recollections of past life experiences. It appears that these souls are ready for a new way of being on Earth in the new Era.

Given the freedom-loving, sovereign nature of Aquarius, the long-standing rules, regulations and mechanisms of control currently in place on Earth will be revisited. While most of these were sustainable and perhaps even helpful throughout the Era of Pisces, there are many that will not work in the new Era. This will be the case with any and all rules and regulations that are not based on fact or science, or that may deprive one of the basic freedoms of being, choice, creation and expression. Note that rules are not all bad. For example, obeying a traffic signal may save a life or two. But rules that limit freedom of expression will certainly not be tolerated. While change is initially being implemented, there will likely be a tug-of-war between those who desire to maintain control through the old systems, and those who are abandoning their powerlessness, boldly requesting freedom and sovereignty and expressing the desire to create new structures for life on Earth.

The important question will be: Which aspect of the self is requesting freedom? Or, which aspect of the self is seeking to maintain control? Is it the adventurous soul who wants to continue to play in the forest and do as it wills in this make-believe game of separation while remaining oblivious to the fact that it is an integral aspect of creation? Is it the adventurous soul who wants to maintain control over this make-believe world, fearful of the change that is unavoidable during this time of transition? Or will it be the Divine

Self, or Higher Self, the one who remembers the truth of who and what we are, the one who says, "Listen, you are so much more. It's time to come Home now where you will truly be free, where there will be no more fear, no more need to control, no more loneliness and no more lack of any kind." Which voice will you listen to?

This is where firsthand knowledge will take precedence over information derived from outside sources. There is no denying the power and importance of firsthand experience. With each new experience, inner knowing shifts; as knowing shifts, it is easier to adjust and accept change. We can then begin to bridge that gap that has separated us from our Source, the gap that sustains our apparent existence in separation. In order to do this, it will be necessary for us to reunite with a long-lost aspect of ourselves, the part of us that knows that we have never been, nor could ever be separate from Source: our Divine, original Self, the One That Was before getting lost in the forest. As this is a new concept for most, it may take a bit of work, probably more than we'd like. But then again, we want something new, right? We're ready for change, right? And if we truly want the new, then we will need to drop the old and be ready to accept some truly new and perhaps even unimaginable perspectives.

> What you are dealing with in the moment is most real, yes. But even in that occurrence there has been an instant where you have seen that there was another way of looking at it, another way in that instant of seeing that brother as your brother, that one as your sister, that one as your Self. (Jeshua Online—Daily Message)

Taking a Step Back

So it is that while we are now standing in that tiny window of transition between the Eras of Pisces and Aquarius, we have the opportunity to explore, discover, experience and inspire great change for humanity. This tiny window will remain open until the next Era has been fully designed and structured, until new laws, rules and regulations have been firmly put into place. There is no official calendar date for this change to occur, it has not been predetermined, nor will it be dropped on us from "on high." Since today is a result of decisions made in the past, and the future will be a result of decisions made today, all that matters is the present moment.

Change will emerge as a result of decisions that we—as a collective, as a family—make today. This is why it is all the more important that right now we do as much work as we can to activate and expand our awareness of our innate divinity. In so doing, we will contribute to the raising of the consciousness of the human collective so that the world we are creating, the world that will unfold in the new Era will be truly wonderful for all life on Earth. We have the opportunity now to express our true nature as Source Energy Beings and create a world of balance, harmony, inclusiveness, abundance, safety, beauty, creativity, peace, curiosity and above all, love for all.

If we are going to move forward and become free of past limitations, if we are going to claim the more of who and what we are, if we are going to create a new world, we will need to consider that maybe, just maybe there is another way of looking at things. Our newly-conceived stories of our origins, while not factual, may contain elements of truth as they were likely inspired by the Divine Child in us, that still small voice that remembers the truth. My story of the adventurous souls who ran off into the forest and your story of how we lost our way, while unverified and unproven, while not approved by some "expert," might be far more helpful than we realize.

These stories may very well provide the alternative perspective that will allow us to stand back and see things differently. No longer bound by the limitations and distractions of long-standing beliefs, memories and familiar ways of doing things, we will be more open to considering alternatives—even radically new alternatives. Besides, aren't our long-standing beliefs also built on stories? And, who created those stories? Who has been telling and embellishing those stories for thousands of years? Are they relevant, and most of all, helpful today? So, why not make up our own, just to have some new ground on which to stand while we prepare to step forward into the unknown.

CHAPTER 8 · REUNIFICATION

Creating new stories and finding language that does not carry old and especially limiting meanings, meanings that are contrary to the nature of the new world we wish to create, may be very helpful during this time of transition. In my experience, having replaced the early childhood notion of a judging, fierce, punishing man-god with the idea of Pure Life, the Source of All that functions on a foundation of balance, harmony, inclusiveness, peace, respect, curiosity and above all Love made all the difference in the world for me. It was then possible to establish a close relationship with God, something I had only experienced in very brief moments. Pure Life was a new term for me, a term that held no prior definitions or attributes or meanings. I was then able to not only look within but also without and appreciate that Source, Pure Life or God was All in All since it is the Source or the Creator of all that exists. There was indeed another way of looking at everything and it was so much greater than the old way; in fact it was beyond words.

What really surprised me was how this simple change of wording or language could have such a huge impact on, not only my understanding or perception of God, but also on my capacity to trust and have faith in this Source, as it had completely different attributes from the God of my childhood. It could not stir up fear, doubt or concern for my ultimate well-being. Plus, I knew that I was no longer alone. Now, whenever I read about God or hear the word God in an audiobook, I smile. This new God—Pure Life—is inspiring, loving, and I am filled with wonder and awe when I take the time to reach out to it. I feel safe, but especially, I feel loved, and I can't get enough of it.

Oddly, such was not the case with the French word for God I was taught in my childhood: "dieu," or "le bon dieu," the good god, which illustrates the importance of evaluating language. Not having found a suitable word in French, I had to consciously switch it out for Pure Life several times before it lost the old traditional attributes of a fearful, judging, man-god. Maybe it's best to forget the words and just stick with the feeling you get when you reach out and connect with that infinite, loving, flowing Source of Pure Life, that overwhelming feeling of safe, warm, nurturing, joyful Love. Pure Life—God Life; God Love; God Light. Yes. This is the God I now know. This is the God I want to be with every minute, of every day, well, at least once I have removed all the remaining garbage that stands in the way. Did you think it would be that easy? Indeed, there is still work to be done, but knowing what I now know, I can't wait for the full experience. Wherever I am God is; wherever I am is an opportunity to know God in expression, in everything, in every person I encounter. What a gift!

To create a language and imagery that makes us feel at ease may very well be what helps us take a step back, look at things from a different perspective, one that stands on love, compassion, understanding, equality, respect, harmony, peace, inclusivity, and perhaps inspires a desire to serve. It takes us out of the long-held, all-too-familiar patterns of comparison, criticism, measurement, competition, fear and judgment. For, if you are truly standing on a foundation of Pure Life, how could you judge, condemn, shame, demean, harm or punish the one who stands before you? How could you not but love the children who got lost in the forest—the brave adventurous souls—our brothers and sisters who chose to incarnate once again on Earth, our brothers and sisters who, even beneath the smiles, are feeling that loss of connection with their Divine Self and are calling out for Love?

One of my favourite places to experience this energy of Pure Life is on the city bus. Yes, not while meditating, while that works too, but on the city bus with a bunch of strangers, who in reality, are not strangers, but are essentially expressions of Pure Life, our brothers and sisters. I love the feeling of calling in those energies of Pure Life, Love and Light, sometimes simply reciting—silently, to myself, of course—God Life, God Love and God Light. Often, I breathe in God Life, then breathe out God Love, or God Light depending on what I feel is needed. I might close my eyes for a moment as the energies fill the bus. If I notice someone who seems to be in need, I send a little more of that Love and Light their way, wrapping the energies around them like a huge loving hug of light.

CHAPTER 8 · REUNIFICATION

I don't need to be looking at them; I don't need to make anyone feel uncomfortable. I can simply do this while looking out the window.

This is what I did one day for the grumpy bus driver who beeped his horn as an oncoming driver turned his car across the lane in front of the bus. Sensing that he was in need of a little extra help, I sent a wave of warm, loving light in his direction, enveloping him in a warm hug of Pure Life. He couldn't see me, as I was sitting a few seats behind him on the left side of the bus. Once wrapped in that energy of Pure Love, I was not surprised when he started to slow down, his driving now more relaxed. However, I was surprised when a man of a certain age, sitting ahead of me on the right side of the bus, started to stand up at each stop to show new passengers to their seats. "Here's an empty seat," he said as he directed a newcomer to their seat. For a split second, he glanced in my direction and smiled. He had picked up that beautiful energy of Pure Life and was enjoying sharing it with others. My heart swelled as I looked out the window and sent him an armful of that loving energy.

Interestingly, while I was working on this section, I had to chuckle as I read the daily message from Jeshua where I found the same idea I had been using in my writing. Again, I don't know if these are coincidences, or perhaps confirmations, but I just love the synchronicity, as it makes me feel supported on this journey into what appears to be unknown territory, but which is really a return to our true Knowing of who and what we are as expressions of Pure Life. Thank you Jeshua for standing by our side, and thank you Judith Coates for transmitting these messages.

> As you gift yourself the degree of objectivity, being able to stand back and be the Beholder, you can empathize with the feelings. You know them well, but you can also get a grasp, an insight, which happens in an instant, of the larger picture. And if you will receive it, you can see Love even in the midst of conflict. (Jeshua Online—Daily Message)

Finding the Perfect Partner

After realising the importance of self-love, the next big step was reknowing God. That was probably the biggest step on my life-long journey. Then came another step: completion. No, this does not mean completing the book, or completing the learning of a piece of music, or completing a recipe in the kitchen. It's a term that came to me while I was trying to comprehend the process of healing the great divide, the separation from God. There is much talk today about Ascension and enlightenment or becoming your Higher Self, Christ Self, or Divine Self. These terms generally refer to the process we are presently experiencing as we seek to reunite with that aspect of ourselves that was lost when we—as the adventurous souls—ventured out into the forest and forgot about our true origins.

For me, the term Higher Self worked well, as it gave me hope that I could achieve something greater than my familiar small self. But it still carried a sense of distance. There was the old me down here, and a Higher Self up there, somewhere. How high did I need to climb? How small was I? Could I make it? Did I have what I needed to reach my Higher Self? Did I deserve it? Let's just say that I was getting a little tired of what seemed like a never-ending uphill journey.

The small self or separated self is also referred to as the ego in *A Course in Miracles* as well as in many other teachings today. However, I have noticed that the term "ego" can arouse a certain amount of condescension or judgment. It is often perceived as something bad, or sinful and often attracts disparagement or condemnation. "Oh, he's such an ego!" Or, "The ego made me do it." It can also be discouraging, even disempowering for the soul seeking to know the truth of who and what it is. "I'm just an ego. What do I really know? How could I possibly even think of myself as a Christ, let alone a Divine Being!" If there is one essential attribute of Pure Life it is that it does not judge, condemn or demean any of its Creations. It can only love, for that is its true nature. So, if I find myself judging another for functioning from their ego, then I am choosing to not be in alignment with Pure Life, which is contrary to what I deeply desire. I can then accept to learn from this experience and choose to do differently next time. It's a lesson learned, and life on Earth is indeed a great school!

The reference to those "adventurous souls" who got lost in the forest was used throughout this book to avoid the negative or demeaning responses that might be evoked when referring to the small self, or ego. I have found it much easier to accept, forgive and feel love for an "adventurous soul" rather than for an "ego." An adventurous soul is easier to connect with Pure Life than that "guy" who did such a nasty thing, or that "woman" who was such a bitch. Can you reach into your heart once you have labelled someone a narcissist? The term "adventurous soul" makes it easier to see a child in need of love and compassion, while the term "ego" is less likely to stir up loving thoughts, at least in my experience. Here again, we see the importance of language.

Another common term found in spiritual and metaphysical teachings is "ascension," which again carries a sense of a long ride home—a very long journey, from what I was taught, one that can last hundreds of lifetimes. Given my innately impatient nature, and perhaps some frustration with repeated incarnations, it was not a term that inspired me, so it is not a term I have used for myself. Keeping in mind that language is coloured by personal experience, indoctrination and history, each one needs to clean up their own vocabulary, sometimes even replacing old words with words that have not been used before, or just making up new words. Language is a tool for communication, and it reveals what we are attempting to communicate. This is something else we can pay attention to.

A couple of popular terms these days are "enlightened" and "awake." These terms tend to carry many meanings. Some think that being able to quote a spiritual text or rigorously engaging in a spiritual practice makes them enlightened. This may indicate a form of specialness, something that an adventurous soul thrives on. "I practice meditation every day and I can quote this book word for word! I'm enlightened!" But then they will look down at the unenlightened souls, the ones who do not engage in the same practices or read the same books. What they do not realize is that the truly enlightened soul does not see hierarchies or specialness; it does not judge or condemn. The truly enlightened soul knows how very little it actually knows, and above all, it knows that all are of God, regardless of their practices or beliefs.

Some will claim that in order to be truly enlightened or awake you need to know everything that's going on in the world, especially all that is dark, negative and corrupt. But that only makes them an expert in that which is dark, negative and corrupt. "If you're not aware of the horrible things that are going on, then you're asleep!" Again, this is a position of condemnation and judgment, and does not reflect the love, compassion and deep understanding of Pure Life. Are they aware of how many people are working on their healing and practicing being at peace and expressing love and compassion for life on Earth?

One might ask: how much darkness do we need to explore before the light begins to shine? Does darkness have an end? Will exploring darkness bring in the light? Isn't the best way to eliminate darkness to simply turn on the light? And where is that light? Well, the light is inside each and every one of us, and it's up to us to go inside, find that switch and turn it on. So, while your function in this life may be to help remove the darkness, don't forget to turn on your light when doing your work.

While I liked the terms becoming whole or claiming the Higher Self, Divine Self, or Christ Self, I needed something that would help bring my small self, the adventurous soul, in alignment with this Higher Self. This is where the term "complete" came to me. Becoming complete was like joining two pieces of a puzzle—two pieces that were designed to fit together perfectly. It was like the perfect marriage we seek in the world, which may be the true motivation behind our search for that "perfect" partner or that "better half." "I want to find someone who completes me." Only now, we are discovering that this perfect partner is inside of us, and has

CHAPTER 8 • REUNIFICATION

never left us. It has always been there waiting for us to look inside and say, finally: "Hello, I'm here!"

The term "complete" seemed more accessible, less effortful than climbing a high mountain or travelling to distant dimensions far, far away, or having to endure hundreds of incarnations. All that was needed was to express the desire to become complete once again, to know that this aspect of us has never—could, or would never—abandon us since Pure Life does not reject any of its Creations. Pure Life never divides as it remains always whole and complete. As an aspect of Pure Life, I, you, we remain always complete. The challenge is to accept this strange new notion, and remove any doubts or beliefs that stand in the way of realizing our essential completeness. Now we can say:

> My perfect partner is my Inner Self, my Higher Self, my True Self, or my Christ Self. I am ready to join with my Higher Self now. I welcome my True Self now. And so as I become One with my Christ Self, I am complete.

While I was editing this section—note that I had been working on this chapter for several weeks—my attention was drawn to the opening notes of a piece playing on the classical station. It sounded familiar, so I got up to find out what it was, and of course, it was Beethoven's 9th. Just out of curiosity, I switched over to the other station just to see what was playing. I frequently toggle between the Popular Classical and Classic Masters stations and pick the one I prefer. Well, this was an easy pick. The 3rd movement of Rachmaninoff's Piano Concerto No. 2 had just started. Beethoven would have to wait ten minutes.

As I was pondering this process of becoming complete, the reunification of the small self with the Higher Self, the music kept calling me Home. No matter how much I doubted that this was even possible, it was telling me that I can do this, that we can all do this; we can, each and every one of us, become complete. Completeness is our natural condition as Divine expressions of Source, as children of God, as expressions of Pure Life, Love and Light. This is where the music comes from; this is where we get our insights, our creative urges, our inspiration, and our answers. Everyone has had these experiences; everyone knows what it feels like when the light is turned on! Aha! I see now; I know. Yes, we have every right to desire and claim our completeness, our wholeness, and to experience the truth of who and what we are. This is what we will need to know and experience as we move forward. We must heal our inner brokenness, join our perfect partner—our Christ Self—and become, once again, complete.

And yes, of course the tears flowed, and it felt good. When I changed the channel back to Beethoven's 9th, I sat at the computer, wondering what I could write next. Nothing seemed to matter anymore. What else could be said? Eventually carried by the final movement of this exquisite piece of music, I decided to read through it once more, to see if it needed any tweaks. Yes, I'm a slow writer, and I do lots of rewrites! And yes, as I was editing the writing, I was feeling the music, and I was letting it carry me forward! The following day, I had to laugh when I checked my early morning email. Someone must be spying on me!

> None of you are static. You are very much vibrating and resonating to each other's frequency of vibration. That is why when you hear a piece of music you vibrate with those tones. You can feel the vibration of yourself intermingling and meshing with the vibration of music. (Jeshua Online—Daily Message)

Thank you Jeshua and Judith Coates. We are so blessed with all the help we need. Thank you for answering our calls for help. Thank you, thank you, thank you!

CHAPTER 9

Standing at the Gateway

"*My salvation comes from me.
It cannot come from anywhere else.*"
"*Nothing outside of me can hold me back.
Within me is the world's salvation and my own.*" (ACIM, Lesson 70)

The Saviour Has Come!

If you take a minute to think about the above quote from *A Course in Miracles*, you come to realize that it is quite loaded, maybe even brutal. "You mean it's all up to me? Really? That's impossible! How could that be?" the adventurous soul exclaims. Yet, the information in those few lines alone holds some of the most important keys for the fulfillment of that deep desire for change, for the creation of a beautiful new world of balance, harmony, peace, inclusiveness, compassion, respect and love, but above all, for the healing of our own brokenness and for the release of the fear that ensued once we decided to step away from our true Home and venture out into worlds of our own making.

Throughout *A Course in Miracles*, Jeshua corrects many of the alterations and distortions of his teachings that have emerged over time. In Lesson 70, he clearly sheds light on a long-held misunderstanding of his function on Earth, a misunderstanding that has no doubt contributed to the delay of our return to completeness due to the fact that it turned our attention in the wrong direction: outward rather than inward. Indeed, he came to show his adventurous brothers and sisters the way—not the way to him, but the way

Home, to the Christ within, the Holy Spirit or our True Self. He showed that this could be done through love of self and of others, by choosing forgiveness over judgment and the need for vindication and punishment, and especially by healing the separation from God and reclaiming our Oneness with all of Creation.

Naturally, he used the language of the day so that his message could be more easily understood. At that time, there was a severe imbalance between the male and female energies due to the fact that humanity had just completed a two thousand year trek through the Era of Aries. As the first sign of the zodiac cycle, Aries represents the initial impulse or drive to explore and venture out, and it is fuelled by pure male, or yang energy which can be competitive and aggressive, even violent when out of balance. This is reflected in some of the teachings of the time, from which emerged a rather hostile, judgmental, punitive male God that supported war as well as homicide as a form of punishment.

While Aries carries an energy of autonomy and self-reliance that can inspire great courage and a drive for adventure, it can also strengthen the denial of God, depending on how it is used. A complete, fully aware, Divine Soul will use this energy to aspire for more and explore the new while remaining fully mindful of the impact of its choices on all of Creation. A self-focused adventurous soul, living in denial of its essential connection with God, unaware of its contribution to the whole, will be fundamentally motivated by fear and more likely to use this energy for self-protection or self-gratification, with little or no concern for the impact of its choices and actions on the whole.

Another factor to consider is that during Jeshua's time on Earth, humanity was experiencing the transition between two extremes in the cycle of the Eras, that is, from Aries to Pisces or from the bottom of one ladder to the top of the next. This was a huge, radical leap as the signs grow in complexity from the first to the last. It was as though humanity was offered an opportunity to jump straight to the ultimate destination—a first-class one-way ticket on the express train Home with no stops in between. By skipping over the other ten Eras, the adventurous souls had a direct line to the reknowing of who and what they were as beloved expressions of Pure Life, as integral parts of Creation gifted with access to unlimited potential as Divine Creator Beings. In that critical moment of transition, they had the opportunity to break free and explore what lies beyond their familiar forest playground, to reknow the infinite potentialities available to all as expressions of Pure Life.

At that time, humanity was shifting from an Era that focused on and promoted the separated, self-focused, adventurous soul's journey to an Era that had the most potential to heal the separation and nurture the awareness of the Oneness of Creation. At the start of the Pisces Era, through the works of Jeshua and other teachers, the seeds of unlimited, unconditional love of all and for all were sown through teachings that clearly invited the adventurous souls to reconsider their choice for separation and to know that, while each is unique, all is of Source, and all is of God.

It was time to abandon that unfulfilling, painful denial of God, that lonely, fearful, unnatural state of separation; it was time to embrace the true, Divine Self and reunite with All That Is. It was an opportunity to reknow the balance, harmony, integrity, unity, respect, inclusiveness, compassion, acceptance, wisdom and love with which Pure Life flows. It was a huge leap, clearly, one that most adventurous souls were not quite ready for, one that was chosen by only a very few rare souls. So it is that we find ourselves once again, two thousand years later, facing another opportunity to make that choice, to heal the inner wound and become complete, to reknow ourselves as expressions of Pure Life.

The Course clearly states that we have the power and the freedom within us to accomplish this incredible feat. "*My salvation comes from me. It cannot come from anywhere else.*" If we are ready to accept this fact and, more importantly, act upon it, we will not only be experiencing our own healing, but we will be making a tremendous contribution to the healing of all life on Earth. Again, as freedom is a welcome trait in the new Era, this is something we can aspire to, perhaps even work with. Still, while we may love our freedom, do we really have the power to make such a huge leap? Some might have trouble accepting this point. It seems a bit too farfetched. We can't possibly have that much power!

When the adventurous souls turned their back on God and broke the connection with their True Self, the safety and comfort of Oneness faded. From this state of separation, there emerged a sense of lack and vulnerability, thus establishing a foundation of fear, something that is not known in Pure Life. Once fear set in, something fearful had to be manifested or projected outside to validate that fear. No longer aware of their inherent divinity, they unknowingly continued to express their innate creativity, only now it was projected out into a make-believe world of their own creation, a world of fear, imbalance, lack, greed, competition and struggle at all levels. With a focus on the world outside, the safety of Pure Life that resides always within was effectively abandoned. From the perspective of life in a state of separation from Source, in denial of God, out of desperation and having long forgotten the way Home, they picked up the notion that someone or something outside of them must, and would come and save them. "Help! We need a saviour!"

There are many today who believe that a saviour came to save us two thousand years ago, and he will come again, and he is known as Jesus Christ. These souls are eagerly awaiting his return or "second coming" so they may be saved. They feel confident in this belief, given that this is what they were taught from a very young age. Knowing without a doubt that they will be saved, there is really nothing they need to do. But, if Jesus saved us way back then, why does he need to come back and save us again? Can anyone really save us? Again, saved from what, exactly?

As an illustration of this way of thinking, or this "saviour complex," I crossed paths with a woman, probably around my age, who lives in an apartment building nearby. Every other month or so I see her waiting for the bus as I'm walking home from the grocery store. I stop, we chat a few minutes, or rather she talks and I listen, and then we go our separate ways. These chats generally focus on current events, and her stories often end up with a raised hand and

CHAPTER 9 · STANDING AT THE GATEWAY

a call for help or an expression of gratitude for "le bon dieu," an acknowledgement of the presence and mercy of God.

During the week I was working on this chapter, we crossed paths twice. After the second encounter, I realized that perhaps I was meant to share this story, as it was very much in line with what I was writing about. It was the week after the famous solar eclipse. While both times our conversation began with her asking for my thoughts on the eclipse, it was really just a door opener so she could share her thoughts, or rather her beliefs, on the subject. That was okay, as I was accustomed to these kinds of interactions. She was excited about the eclipse because she believed, without a doubt, that it had been sent by God. The focus of the talk toggled between the devil and the horrible things going on in the world, and her firm belief that God was coming to fix everything. So, from her perspective, there was nothing to worry about. Besides, she only had this one life to live, and when she died she would go straight to Heaven.

How do you have a conversation with someone like that, you might ask? Well, you listen from your heart, you don't argue, you let them be right, because that's what they want, and that's what makes them feel safe and comfortable. It is important to respect a person's boundaries. Most people in my life are not on a "spiritual" journey, at least not consciously. I have learned to just listen and nod in agreement, while waiting for an opportunity to slip in a bit of my perspective, or a story that might fit it, which I only do if I can shape it in a way that will resonate with the one before me. This practice of letting others have their knowing, without pointing out possible—or actual—errors or crossing their boundaries is a helpful approach in the Era of Aquarius. We don't need to be right; we need to be compassionate, inclusive, kind, understanding, supportive and, above all, loving. Plus, I need to be patient, which is probably my biggest lesson in this life. Removing the burden of righteousness is quite a relief, plus it makes interactions with our fellow adventurous souls lighter, oftentimes helpful, and certainly much more fun.

In order to shift the focus of the conversation from the "problem" to the "solution," I slipped in how Jesus had taught the importance of love. She nodded in agreement, but said nothing more. As everyone loves a good story, I took this as an opportunity to share my bus story with her. She was very surprised that sending love might actually have an impact on people. "Love is good," she agreed, but quickly added that she preferred to just pray. Then she returned to her narrative about the evil of humanity and the devil, and then shrugged and said that it was all okay, since she sincerely believed that things were about to change because God would fix everything, and she was at peace with that. I just nodded in agreement, and smiled and then apologized for keeping her from going where she was headed. This time we were not at the bus stop. I was on my way home, and she was on her way to church to pray. And so I wished her a lovely day.

Helping others, rescuing and saving people and animals, even sacrificing oneself for others is very much in line with the core energy of Pisces. Many have experienced a deep sense of joy and fulfillment as well as self-worth through these practices. So it is understandable that at the start of the Era of Pisces, the answer to calls for help would appear as a saviour. This is the best that the long-lost adventurous souls could accept at that time. However, what they did not understand is that it doesn't quite work that way. While help may be offered, the adventurous souls have a part to play—a significant part. To look outside for a saviour perpetuates the error of separation, plus it gives one's power away. Fortunately, this will not be in alignment with the energy of Aquarius. All that is needed is to look within and to recognize our innocent adventure— a momentary detour—into a make-believe world of separation. We need to save ourselves from our choice for and belief in separation. In this way, *we* are the second coming.

Over the last couple of decades, many stories have emerged about help being sent our way. Yet, while some of this information sounded interesting, and perhaps even encouraging, at first I had a bit of trouble accepting, trusting and even believing in saviours and

CHAPTER 9 • STANDING AT THE GATEWAY

helpers of any kind. "I'll stick to self-reliance!" the Aquarius in me declared. Through a rather unusual dream, I came to understand the cause of my reluctance to asking for, trusting and expecting help. Late one night, while deep asleep, I had a dream where I witnessed what appeared to be an intervention of sorts from entities who were attempting to help humanity. They appeared as energy beings or what some might call angels, coming toward us from another dimension, bringing much-needed light to the souls on Earth at the time. Then for some reason, the helper beings stopped and pulled back, thus failing to complete their intervention. I'm not sure when this event occurred; I only had a sense that it was hundreds of years ago, perhaps more. Plus, I'm not very good at remembering dreams. But I do recall feeling let down, even resentful and betrayed for not having been given the help we had asked for.

From what I learned, this was a response meant to counterbalance an undertaking that had been initiated on Earth, something that did not honour the fundamental principles of harmony, respect, balance and unity of Pure Life. In other words, it was meant to correct an inappropriate direction taken by adventurous souls who functioned in separation. This is where I came to understand that there exists a law of non-interference in Creation. Help may be offered, but it must also be received, integrated and acted upon. No one can interfere with the choices made by a Creator Being, even if they are playing the role of childish, adventurous soul and doing so without the slightest idea of who and what they truly are. They can be shown a different way, but this different way must be chosen and accepted and lived. As we are, at our core, Divine Creator Beings, with the freedom to choose how we will use our creative energies, no one can fix things for us. After seeing this, I was able to release the resentment I felt for failed attempts to help humanity, as I also sensed that this was not the first one. There are loving beings that remain always ready to help us find our way Home, but it's on us to do something with that help. We are not helpless babies. Jeshua explains this well in *A Course in Miracles*.

If I merely intervened between your thoughts and their results, I would be tampering with a basic law of cause and effect, the most fundamental law there is in this world. I would hardly help if I depreciated the power of your own thinking. (ACIM, Ch. 2, p. 39)

Ultimately, the only way we can be saved is for us to stand up and acknowledge that we want to know the truth of who and what we are. We must be ready to release the veil of ignorance. But, above all, we must be ready to do whatever it takes to achieve and experience this knowing. Only then will the appropriate help—the help that suits our needs at the moment—be offered and made available. You will know you are being helped and supported because you will feel the love of the ones who offer it to you. And because many are stirring and asking for help, much help is being offered today. All that is needed is to be willing to release the old conditioning, the long-held, no-longer-helpful beliefs, and be open to the new. Remember also that you always have the freedom to choose what you will accept and what you will discard. There is no hurry, nor does it need to be uncomfortable or effortful, as this is a return to our natural condition as expressions of Pure Life, as who and what we were created to be.

And so it was that on a beautiful, sunny, Monday morning, as I settled down to work on this chapter, I was gifted with the inspiration I needed with Mozart's Requiem. Oddly, or perhaps not, it played again on another beautiful, sunny, Monday morning a couple of weeks later while I was editing this very section. Don't get me wrong, I don't choose the music; I just turn on the radio before I get to work. The classical stations I listen to play a wide range of pieces, all day long. It just so happens that certain pieces show up at certain times. Synchronicity? Whatever it is, it makes me feel as though I am a part of something bigger than me, an energetic structure that is far greater than anything I could concoct myself. It is a feeling of belonging, of being a part of the Oneness of Creation, flowing with Pure Life, a feeling that is nearly impossible to describe in words. And no doubt because I needed a little extra boost on this journey that seemed at times overwhelming, the Daily Message was once again just what I needed. Plus, it was completely in line with the next section.

> You are a great energy, a great ray of Light. All of you have agreed that you will be here in this time to remember, to come Home, and to empower yourself; not by outside means, but to empower yourself through remembrance of the power that you are. (Jeshua Online—Daily Message)

Redirecting Faith

Throughout history, Jeshua, as well as many other loving brothers and sisters have come to Earth to help the lost adventurous souls find their way back Home. The teachings are there, in various texts, sometimes buried beneath distracting distortions, at other times completely misunderstood by the adventurous souls who took it upon themselves to advocate them. The truth of our divine origins, our innate wholeness, or holiness, as well as the importance of forgiveness, withholding judgment, the inherent Oneness of Creation and especially love and respect for self, for others and for our home planet has been shared with us from the origins of time. These teachings were given so we could apply them, and thus heal and save ourselves from our condition of separation from Source, from our denial of God. The truth is there, it has never been withheld, and it has always been available for the ones who truly want to know it. Why would Pure Life, the Creator, Source or the loving Mother/Father/God withhold something so important from its beloved creations?

As we enter the Age of Aquarius, an Era that thrives on freedom and sovereignty, this concept of saviour is likely to be easily set aside in favour of a more self-empowered, or self-reliant approach. An "I can do it myself" attitude is rapidly emerging as can be seen by the proliferation of independent social media channels. Since "to know" from personal experience is a basic attribute of Aquarius, it is not surprising that experts in all walks of life are speaking out and sharing their knowledge. In this new Era, it will be pointless to argue or attempt to convert others to your way of thinking, even if you have valid proof for your position. The best approach is to know and let them know.

During the transition to a new world, the old knowing may temporarily serve as a crutch or safety net, providing something to lean on and allowing us to take small, more comfortable steps forward. As consciousness expands and new knowing emerges, much of what we thought we knew is likely to fall by the wayside. Since every soul's journey is unique, in this Era of sovereignty the best expert for us will be our Higher Self, the Divine Child, the Christ within, or whatever term we choose to use for the unseparated, unbroken aspect within that has never forgotten the truth of who and what we are. All the more reason to heal that brokenness and experience completeness so we can access that natural, inner wisdom and expertise.

As many are asking for help during this time of transition, much help is being offered. However this help—true help—may not appear in the desired form. Some adventurous souls are stomping their feet, asking for, even demanding, to get what they want, how they want it and when they want it. "I want that nice house I've been dreaming about for years." "I want that great job I've been working hard for." "I want that perfect partner so I can finally be happy." Would a loving Being, one who was asked for help by a lost child, a lost sibling, not give help? "But I didn't get what I wanted!" Perhaps the child is simply not seeing the help that is being most generously sent as they are still blinded and distracted by their experience as an incomplete, small self, seeking to maintain its adventure behind the veil of separation.

Fortunately, at this time we are experiencing a far less radical leap on the ladder of the Great Year from the Era of Pisces to the Era of Aquarius, so we may be more open to the messages and teachings of the truth of who we are, the truth of our origins. While it is a step down the ladder, Aquarius and Pisces do share, to varying degrees, some basic attributes such as appreciation for community, the vast scope of potentialities on many levels, the desire to learn

CHAPTER 9 • STANDING AT THE GATEWAY

and understand and a curiosity for what lies beyond the boundaries of the known. These common traits may make the transition into the new Era a bit smoother than the more extreme transition between Aries and Pisces. Still, there are traits that are quite different between Pisces and Aquarius, and these are likely to pose challenges for those who wish to cling to the old and are not ready or willing to move forward into the new Era.

What will be helpful on this journey is to have a little faith. However, this faith may be difficult to access at first, since the freedom-loving, sovereign side of Aquarius does not resonate well with faith, at least not the blind faith that became so entrenched in the human experience during the Pisces Era. And since Aquarius likes proof, and tangible proof may not be available yet as we are in the early stages of the transition into a new way of being for humanity, faith will need to be strengthened. If we truly want to transition to a new experience for ourselves and for all life on Earth, we will need to find ways to place our faith in the unknown, in that which has not yet been scientifically validated, measured, tested or proven. We will then need to trust that we will be brought to that new experience we desire in the most graceful way possible.

> There is another vision and another Voice in which your freedom lies, awaiting but your choice. And if you place your faith in them, you will perceive another Self in you. (ACIM, Ch. 21, p. 511)

Many will be challenged, as we have been taught to place our faith outside ourselves, in those in power, from our parents and teachers to the leaders, the "holy" ones and the so-called experts. In order to have the strength and courage needed during this period of great change, we will need to learn to trust our Inner Self, our Higher Self, that still small voice that nudges us along and gives us those priceless gems of wisdom when we are open enough to pay attention and listen to it. In other words, we will need to place our faith inward instead of outward, as has been done since the start of our journey into separation. This will be a new experience for humanity at this time, and no doubt a challenge for many, if not most, and perhaps nearly impossible for some. Fortunately, with the desire for freedom and sovereignty on the rise, the practice of turning inward for insights, healing, confirmation and support will gradually become easier, and at one point it will even become natural.

One of the reasons why it can be helpful to make up our own stories of our origins is that we can then trace our way straight to Source, to our Divine Self, without being held back or distracted by the distortions and limitations of familiar language, imagery, programming and history. Besides, if it is true that at our core we have never been separate from Pure Life or Source, if nothing exists outside of God, then there will be great benefit found in turning inward. How can anything feel better than reconnecting with our long-lost, all-inclusive, non-judgmental, compassionate, loving Source! And since feeling is a natural attribute of Aquarius, this redirection of our attention to something that feels overwhelmingly good will no doubt be facilitated. This again will not be easy at first, as we have been trained to think and to focus our attention outward and to accept and believe what our teachers and leaders have taught. But, with a little faith, there is nothing that stops us from taking a peek inside.

So, how can we strengthen our faith in this unknown Divine Inner Self? First, we must be open to the idea that maybe, just maybe, there is a part of us that remembers who and what we are, that has never forgotten our Divine origins. Expressing as Pure Life, loving, balanced and respectful, knowing what is best for us, this part of us simply stands by, ready to help when we reach out. This will be an important step in achieving our completeness. Once we have accepted this far-out notion, that this is even possible, we can begin to put it into practice in our everyday lives.

One easy way to begin the healing of our inner brokenness is to practice being quiet every now and then, turn our attention inward, connect with that Self and listen. Pay attention to the experience; forget the theory or any fancy theology. Don't think; just listen, and wait for the feeling. It will—and must—feel good, since you will be connecting with more love, more abundance, and more safety than you have ever felt as a separated, small self. This does not mean that you will cut yourself off from the outside world. Quite the contrary. You will simply have a broader base on which to build your experience as you will be "Being" as a complete, True Divine Self, with access to Source, allowing Pure Life, Pure Love and Pure Light to naturally flow and express as you.

Whenever you have a question, ask it of your Inner Self first. When considering information or a situation that comes from outside, run it by your Inner Self. Everyone is familiar with insights; everyone has had a thought—a flash—that provided an answer to what seemed like an unresolvable issue. These flashes very often occur once you have stopped attempting to find the answer through thinking. You were unable to resolve a problem, so you gave up; you decided to focus on something else, something completely unrelated. Then, out of nowhere, the answer or the solution somehow just popped into your mind. "Why didn't I think of that before!" In that moment, a connection was made with your Inner Self, your Christ Self. You were in fact not thinking!

At times, you may also find that something outside of you confirms what your Inner Self revealed to you, in this way, strengthening your faith in your Self. This frequently happens to me while I'm listening to an audiobook. For example, I may be washing a cup in the kitchen sink while the voice in the audiobook mentions "holding a cup in hand." Or, I turn to the clock on the stove at exactly 11:11. The number 11 for me represents the antennas used to connect within. I have experienced so many of these "coincidences" that now, I just chuckle. Many are increasingly familiar with these coincidences or synchronicities. The "universe" or Pure Life does respond to us as we are all integral parts of Creation. Of course, it was not surprising when, the morning after writing the first draft of this section, this message appeared in my Inbox:

> As you build an awareness of totality of Self, you will find a grand variety of expression of your Self available instantly. You will find a strength that will protect you throughout all

challenges, a strength that you did not even know you had. (Jeshua Online—Daily Message)

Unveiling the Gateway

So, where is this mysterious, magical Gateway anyways? What does it look like? How do we reach it? Is it in some distant galaxy, far, far away? What if we can't find it or what if we can't make our way through it? Does it require lifetimes of prayer and self-abnegation and repentance for our countless sins? What if we don't deserve it! We'll never make it! What if it doesn't even exist? Okay, I think I'll need a shot of Rachmaninoff to get started on this topic!

Why would this not be an easy topic to address? Isn't it what we've all been waiting for? Don't we want to go through this gateway so we can finally be free? The challenge is that it inevitably puts us face-to-face with some issues that can no longer be ignored, issues that have hindered our healing, our progress, our ability to reclaim the truth of our Being for aeons. Why would these issues be a problem? For various reasons, ranging from fear of the unknown to resistance to change and unwillingness to release long-held, familiar ways of doing and being. "Do I really want to 'be' more than what I have been? I'm tired. Life has been hard enough already!" And then, maybe there are benefits to maintaining the old, benefits we are not yet ready to release. "My life has been very fulfilling; I've worked hard for everything I have, I don't want to lose it." "I have everything I've always wanted. I don't need anything more."

However, challenges shouldn't be too much of a problem since beings in the human condition on Earth have been overcoming hurdles since the beginning of time in separation. We are accustomed to living with challenges of all sorts, and we even derive great pleasure from and even highly value these challenges. Some firmly believe that challenges are necessary to truly thrive. "Hey, I need something to challenge me so I can be strong, so I can really be good!" In fact, some will see life without obstacles as boring. So, what's one more challenge?

CHAPTER 9 • STANDING AT THE GATEWAY

While we may not necessarily want more of what we have experienced, or more of who we have been in this life, we are growing curious and may even be ready to experience something beyond the known, beyond the familiar. There is that still small voice deep inside that is calling us, inviting us to remember who we were before we became adventurous souls, lost in a world of our own creation. Yes, we are the adventurous souls, a term I like so much better than "sinners" who were kicked out of the Garden of Eden, or "mere mortals" or "humans" who evolved from apes, or beings who were genetically modified to serve as slaves for some highly advanced extraterrestrial entities. It makes it easier to look at someone and see them as an innocent child of God who has simply lost its way, to look at them without judgment but more importantly, with love. This is exactly what is needed here on Earth at this time if we want to create a new world: a new way of looking and seeing, a new way that sees beyond history, beliefs, memory and teachings, a new way which must include seeing through the eyes of the Heart.

So let's examine some of the challenges that might be encountered as we transition from Pisces to Aquarius. First, there is great fear of the unknown, which is understandable since this is what is taught in most of our stories. If you watch a science fiction movie or read a book about the future you will see scary beings and aliens ready to attack and kill those who dare to venture out where no man/woman has gone before. What if the new—the unknown—is far worse than what we have now? What if we cannot control or manage it? What if it is more powerful than us? At least we know how to protect and defend ourselves in this familiar world. Maybe we should wait until we know more. Let's wait for science to figure it out.

Throughout history, standing on a foundation of fear, lack and vulnerability, the adventurous souls have faced the unknown, weapons in hand, ready for war, expecting danger and threats to their very survival. This is the life that the adventurous souls created for themselves in the state of separation from Source. It was only natural that they would project this fear and readiness for war beyond their familiar domain, onto the unknown, in any form it might take. Had they maintained their connection with Pure Life, living in a state of harmony, balance, respect, compassion and love for all life, they would have imagined—and attracted—a kinder, more inviting unknown.

In traditional teachings, fear was further strengthened through beliefs in punishment for sin. When you die, you will be judged, and according to your behaviour and the gravity of your sins and errors, you will be mildly punished or severely punished. You must return to Earth and pay for your bad karma. And so it is that fear is probably the most powerful driving force for adventurous souls living in separation from Source. Then of course, there is the belief that we are just mere bodies, living in a material world, vulnerable to forces beyond our control. If something happens to the body, you cease to exist. However, with more and more stories emerging about near-death experiences as well as past-life memories, the view of life being limited to a linear, 3D, physical timeline is beginning to shift.

There may also be some benefits to maintaining fear in our stories. On the one hand, it allows the eager adventurous souls, the ones who like to pretend they have power over the less empowered to maintain control. This can only be a pretend power—an illusion of power—for, how can one being have power over Pure Life in expression? Plus, as they are living in denial of God, they too are standing on a foundation of fear. What if there was no one over which they could hold power? Since this is only an illusory power, would they then feel powerless?

On the other hand, the sustaining of fear allows the ones who have rejected their essential power—or have actually temporarily set it aside—to follow the rules and dictates without the need to question or think and decide for themselves. To be disempowered is also a choice. They can then conveniently blame someone or something outside themselves for their poor choices, or difficult situations. Functioning on a foundation of fear, their actions are more reactive than proactive, or unconscious rather than conscious. "It's not my fault. They made me do it. I had no choice."

CHAPTER 9 • STANDING AT THE GATEWAY

It is becoming evident that in the Era of Aquarius, fear will not likely be sustained, because it just doesn't feel good, and Aquarius is very much about the feeling. Plus, with the attribute of sovereignty kicking in, fewer adventurous souls will be opting to hand over their power. As more and more souls are becoming sensitized to the importance of Oneness, harmony and inclusiveness, the balance of power will shift to one that will serve all life on Earth. It appears that the universal, all-encompassing energies of Pisces may have been too great a leap for those experiencing the transition from Aries to Pisces. However, the far less radical shift from Pisces to Aquarius will support a more loving, compassionate, humanitarian, community-centred world.

The concept of facing the unknown—or at least too much unknown—will likely be challenging as it is contrary to the mind-set of knowing, and to know is foundational in the Era of Aquarius. Plus, those who are regaling in the knowing energies of Aquarius will not necessarily be comfortable or happy with the idea of learning something new. "I know enough; I don't need to learn anything more." Being knowledgeable provides a certain sense of comfort, perhaps even security, and most of our traditional teachings, cultures and educational institutions give us some form of familiar knowledge about who and what we are. These teachings have been accepted, mostly without question, by adventurous souls choosing to journey in separation. Accepting what is taught without question, requires less effort than asking questions for which there does not seem to be any answers. Again, in this new Era, firsthand experience, actual facts and valid data will result in the release of ideas and teachings that are no longer suitable. This may help open the door to the unknown, allowing new knowing to emerge and replace the old.

Since we have long forgotten what it is like to be in unity, that we are part of the Oneness of Creation, we have adapted to living in separation. In separation, we have abandoned our inner authority. We must find authority somewhere. Again, we find it outside of ourselves. The implications of that state of separation are far greater than anything else we could experience because it is then projected outside into the world. In so doing, we effectively turn away from the Source of our Life, the Source of who and what we are, the Source of our creative potential.

Once established in separation, the idea was then projected out into the world of our creation. The concept of duality is the source or cause of what ails humanity in all ways. Duality in and of itself is not bad, nor is it sinful. Tall-short, day-night, dark-light, hot-cold, male-female, Creator-created are simply different aspects of the movement of creation, or two sides of the same coin. In other words, all facets remain part of the Whole. The problem arose when we became divided, or believed ourselves to be completely separate from our Source. In our need for self-protection, this duality was expressed as good vs bad, positive vs negative, empowered vs disempowered, haves vs have-nots. That level of duality is what creates all of our problems. Rising above duality does not mean the loss of uniqueness or individuality, nor does it mean the loss of variety. Oneness does not mean the disappearance of you. All differences and variations are honoured and respected in Oneness, again, an essential attribute of Pure Life.

What can be helpful in making this renewed connection with our Source is to understand that this separation experience was just an experiment. It's like experimenting with a new recipe in the kitchen. Maybe you added too much flour and the bread didn't rise well. It's no big deal. The same is true with our life decisions and choices, both successes and misses. The Source cannot and will not judge or punish us. Those are attributes of fearful separated individuals in the human condition. Only separated beings judge, condemn and seek retribution. The infinite Source has neither reason nor need to judge since it knows that it is infinite, unbreakable, eternal and above all loving, and it has gifted its creations with the same attributes. All that is needed is that we reclaim these attributes for ourselves as expressions of Pure Life, as children of God.

The fact that the separation experience was simply the result of a choice made by the adventurous souls to wander off and explore on their own is not something that has been taught. Instead, we were

CHAPTER 9 • STANDING AT THE GATEWAY

taught that we sinned, disobeyed a command of God and got kicked out of the Kingdom of Heaven. Right away, this teaching reveals that it cannot be correct, or even remotely true, as what God creates is like itself, therefore it could not sin. The creations—or children of God—are free to explore, experiment and experience unlimited adventures, but that does not make them sinners. The idea of sin can only come from a foundation of fear of punishment. It cannot come from God.

Another challenge is to accept that we freely chose to explore life apart from Oneness, in denial of God, separate from Source. We chose life in separation, and we agreed to live as though it were possible. We have the experience of our choosing. We have always been and remain always free to choose. Again, this idea may be challenging, at least at first, because it requires that we then accept the consequences of our choices. The next challenge is to accept responsibility for our choices, for our agreement to life in separation. To be accountable for our thoughts, actions and choices, will have significant consequences. There are certain benefits to being a victim of powers outside of us. What may make this easier to accept is to keep in mind that this choice for, and agreement to an experience of life in separation from Source could only be a fantasy, or an illusion, for nothing or no one can exist outside of the Oneness of Pure Life.

So, where is this Gateway? The Gateway Home to the loving Pure Life Creator is here, now, in the moment. It has always been here, and it has never been withheld from us. How could access to Pure Life be withheld from its creations? But, how do I access this Gateway for myself? And, what perfect timing as the glorious finale of Rachmaninoff's Second Piano Concerto fills the air, the piece of music that says so boldly, yes, this is it, we can do it!

Try this: stand in front of a mirror. Take a couple of deep breaths. Don't look at the defects, the wrinkles, the messy hair. Just breathe. Now, connect with your heart, breathe, and then look into your eyes. Feel that love for yourself, you know, that love you felt when holding your child or favourite pet. Breathe. Feel it. Let the love push those tears into your eyes. Once you feel that love, that love for the brave, courageous one you are for embarking on this journey, you will be ready for the answer.

The Gateway to a new humanity is *you*, *me* and each and every being. Billions of souls have agreed to come to Earth at this time, to come together and release the past so we can begin to rise above the ancient, diminished human condition and create something new, something far greater than what has been known on Earth for far too long. When you have experienced that moment of indescribable fullness, that deep, overwhelming sense of relief, the joy that comes when you accept the truth of who and what you are, you will feel immeasurable gratitude for having been bold enough to reach for the Divine in you.

CHAPTER 10

Sowing the Seeds

Today the time of light begins for you and everyone. It is a new era, in which a new world is born. The old one has left no trace upon it in its passing.… Today we will accept the new world as what we want to see. We will be given what we desire. (ACIM, Lesson 75)

We Journey Not Alone

Why am I still writing? I wondered. It's not like my books are really popular. After having switched from astrology and numerology to writing about my spiritual journey, my publisher was no longer interested in my books. I tried to find another publisher, but none were interested. "Don't worry," my Guides replied. "It will get out to the one who needs it!" I had to chuckle and shake my head. *The one who needs it.* Yes, of course, I knew exactly who *that* was. Yes. I'm the one who needs it, and I will most likely continue to gather notes and insights in my journal. Writing—even the endless rewriting part—has been most helpful throughout my life as it turns my attention inward, where it needs to be. Maybe another soul or two might benefit from my works, and that will be my gift to them. So, yes, thank you for pointing that out. "Oh," they added, "and have fun with it." Okay, maybe writing can be fun, sometimes, but still, it's a lot of work, especially the editing and book production part!

Then when I asked why it was that I seemed to be getting fewer messages from my Guides for this work as compared to some of my earlier books, I was told that much of the guidance I am now receiving is from my own Higher Self. "It is the One who remembers who and what you are, the One who walks with us, that has been answering many of your questions." Wow! Okay, now that made sense as at times I didn't even recognise who I was anymore. Oddly enough, not knowing who I was, or giving up the old self, actually felt good. There was another Self to be discovered, and I found that to be inspiring, even exciting. There was more to me—so much more to be experienced. This shift to a new way of being—to an experience of completeness—was beginning to look like a very real possibility, and it felt especially liberating. I was beginning to have someone else to rely on other than my tired, thinking, fear-based, separated, small self.

While having friends and Guides on this journey is very helpful—actually, we probably wouldn't make it without their help—the most important partner is our Higher Self, the Christ Self, the One that truly knows our needs. Although our Guides will always be with us, ultimately we must stand up and claim the truth of who and what we are, give up who we thought we were, and reconnect with our Higher Self. This is a step only we can take; no one can or will do it for us. Then we will begin to know ourselves as complete Divine expressions of Pure Life, the children of God we have always been.

During this period of shift between Eras, while the old is being dismantled and the new has not yet been established, we have the opportunity to reconnect with our Inner, Higher Self. If we can accept this key point, that there is more to us than what we have known and experienced for a very long time, then we may very well be on our way to creating that beautiful new world we desire. Just to underscore this point, on one of the many mornings I was working on this chapter, the finale of Beethoven's Ninth was playing on the radio. Then a couple of weeks later, while editing this very section, there it was, only this time, starting from the beginning. It's strange how the music appears just in time to punctuate my words. Here it was, boldly and clearly saying that yes, we can stand up and reclaim our essential Divinity. It is available right here, right now. And as I took a pause from writing to bathe in the beautiful

CHAPTER 10 • SOWING THE SEEDS

music, I wiped away the tears. I thought I was done with the tears but this kind of magnificence—the expression of the Divine Inner Voice of the composer—will always move me. It shows us that we are indeed so much more than what we have believed ourselves to be—so much more.

As we move forward to a new, fuller, more complete way of Being, it will be helpful but, most of all, wholly natural for us to develop relationships with our Guides. For those who are relishing the freedom, independence, autonomy, self-reliance and sovereignty of Aquarius, know that accepting a little help from our Guides, those who never forgot who we are as Source Energy Beings, will not diminish any of that—quite the contrary. They understand and work with the principles of Pure Life, and so they will never interfere or impose anything on us as they respect our freedom of choice. Therefore it's okay, and even very wise to ask for help. What if, by asking for help, you were offered insights that made the journey easier? Easier sounds nice, as Aquarius doesn't like overly-inflated complication, drama and complexity. That kind of help would be most welcome!

Our teachers and Guides, our beloved helpers, are inviting us—the adventurous souls—to rise to their level of Being, which is also where that long-forgotten part of us—our Higher Self, our Christ Self—has always been. The truth is that our Higher Self has never been withheld from us, for how could a loving Creator deny essential wholeness and divinity from its Creations? Our Guides, our helpers, want us to break the old habit of placing certain beings on pedestals while remaining small, disempowered and insignificant. That is not the truth of who we are. As we mend our brokenness, as we reconnect with the True Self in us and become complete, as we dare to claim our essential Divinity as expressions of Pure Life, we walk in harmony with our teachers and Guides.

Many souls are now eager to experience the more that has been promised, so they are actively searching for knowledge, solutions, answers and insights. They sincerely desire the experience of being in a new way in the world. Their devotion to this quest naturally draws to them those teachings that provide the answers and the help they need. With the advent of the Age of Aquarius, technologies of all sorts have emerged. This makes it easier for our non-separated brothers and sisters, those who are not bound by the limitations of the physical dimension, to reach out and provide us with the answers to the questions we are asking. This is certainly much easier to do today than it was during Jeshua's life on Earth 2000 years ago. Plus, to facilitate the sharing of the teachings that are needed at this time, many of our brothers and sisters have agreed to serve as channellers for these helpers, so we are indeed blessed with much help.

Through these new messages and teachings, we are gifted with information that is relevant and helpful at this time, so there is no need to spend a lifetime sifting and sorting through ancient teachings that may no longer be relevant. The key is to find those teachings that are at the level and in the language that resonates with us individually. Those are the teachings that will facilitate our return to our Divine origins, or the remembering of who and what we are. We remain always free to accept the information we feel we can handle at the moment, or we can set it aside for later. No one will force this upon us. It remains always our choice.

Also, keep in mind that it's okay to change the language as needed. If there is one thing I have found to be completely mind-altering and very liberating during this lifelong search was to change the language. Changing up the imagery of the Creator and the origins of life, even if this involved a simple made-up story, allowed me to release ancient, limiting perspectives and then to see teachings—to see the world—in a completely new way. This was among the most important steps on my journey, as it opened the doorway allowing me to apply what I was learning in everyday life. Again, practical application and first-hand experience is the only way to access true knowing, a fine trait of Aquarius.

> Truth can only be EXPERIENCED. It cannot be described, and it cannot be explained. (ACIM, Ch. 8, p. 186)

CHAPTER 10 • SOWING THE SEEDS

In order to deal with the overabundance of information being generated today, we can always test it by how it makes us feel. Does it feel right? Is it uplifting? Does it make you curious to know more? Is it inspiring? Does it resonate with, or perhaps confirm an insight you recently had? Does it make you feel stronger, more confident? Does it make you want to reach out and discover the more of who and what you are? Does it fill you with a sense of gratitude? Does it relieve you of uncertainty, anger, resentment, fear or doubt? These types of questions will be entirely appropriate in the Era of Aquarius where you will want to experience the joy of discovery, true knowing, freedom, healing and growth.

I was guided to share this little story, as it was already in the notes for this chapter, just waiting for another edit, but I didn't know where to insert it, or if I should insert it at all. What was fun about this story was, again, the confirmation in the daily message from Jeshua. Even if the journey seems difficult and nearly impossible at times, it does not mean that it can't be fun!

I woke up one morning and as I was getting up and putting my feet on the carpet next to the bed, it occurred to me that I Am, that I am not just this body, there is far more to who and what I am. It is like the body is just a garment, a covering, allowing us to be visible here in this dimension, but there is far more beyond that garment, standing right behind me, above me. It felt like I extended beyond the body, like a cloud of energy. This experience made me feel less impatient with the limiting boundaries of being in a body. It actually made me feel more caring and loving towards it. It has a function here in the world. It allows me to learn, grow and serve in this time of change. Then, when I reached my workspace and checked my inbox, I had to chuckle as I read the Daily Message.

> When you get up and put the foot upon the floor, whose foot do you put upon the floor? Be aware it is the foot of the Christ that you put upon the floor. It is not just the small foot of one human personality. You have seen yourself as one small individuality for long enough. (Jeshua Online—Daily Message)

As I was editing the final chapters of this book, another interesting "coincidence" occurred. I was disappointed because my attempts at obtaining permission to use brief excerpts from some of the songs mentioned had been unsuccessful. In the end, I concluded that the reader could easily find the songs online if they were interested in the lyrics. Then, early one morning, my friend Lise from down the hall knocked on my door. She was coming to get her cat Buckskin before she left for work, or so I thought. An early riser like me, Buckskin had become my daily writing buddy. Well, he lies down on the desk next to me, purrs and then waits to be petted while I work. Maybe he is more of a writing distractor than a writing buddy, especially when he decides to climb on my lap, claw into my belly and butt his nose in my face. But I love his company just the same!

That morning however, Lise wasn't there just for Buckskin. While holding a couple of sheets of paper in her hand, she asked if I wouldn't mind reading over the English version of the lyrics for a song she had just written. Lise (Lyse) Carrier is a wonderful singer and songwriter, but as she writes in French, she likes to make the lyrics available in English for those who want to understand the song. And for good reason, as her songs carry deep messages. "No problem," I said. "I'll look at it later when I'm done with writing." Of course, this was said in French.

Later that day, I sat down and began to read the lyrics. While not entirely surprised by the depth and passion of the message, I was not expecting to be reading the lyrics of a song that cries out what I had been sharing throughout this book. The title of the song was "Qui suis-je?", "Who Am I?" I couldn't believe what I was reading. The song was filled with those questions I had been addressing in my writing. "Am I dream or reality? Who am I? Am I Love? Am I human or a chimpanzee? Or instinct or divinity?" By the time I was done, I was shaking my head. Unbelievable! It was as though she had read my manuscript while I wasn't looking! And yes, this time I was given permission to share the lyrics of this beautiful song, a song that clearly expresses that deep desire to know the more of who and what we are. Merci, Lise.

I have come to understand synchronicities or coincidences as more than mere accidents. Our daily encounters are very much in alignment with our energies, our state of mind, or our vibration. Hence, all the more reason to be vigilant for our thoughts, feelings, emotions, and our motivations for doing what we do throughout the day. For example if you are feeling grumpy, you are likely to encounter someone who will push those grumpy buttons, thus justifying that grumpiness. If you cannot love yourself, if you blame yourself, feel shame and guilt or make yourself small in any way, you will have to project that outside of yourself. You will then encounter someone or something that will justify those thoughts and feelings. We project what we don't want to deal with, and we attract what can be used as learning opportunities.

On the other hand, if you are feeling that love in your heart wanting to come out and express itself, you are likely to encounter someone in need of love, and so you will have an opportunity to share it with that one in need. If you have something to share, something to give, you will very likely cross paths with someone who can benefit from what you have to give. This calls attention to the fact that we are not just adventurous souls living in physical bodies separate from everything and everyone outside of us. We are not alone. We are a part of something far greater. We are One with all of Creation, and that Oneness speaks to us, it communicates with us every moment of every day.

The Birth of a New World

Although I really enjoyed and especially appreciated much of the new information and teachings being shared with us, I had occasional doubts about this wonderful new world we were apparently creating. When reading or listening to messages that praised our progress and how well we are doing on Earth, sometimes I would frown, even cringe. I'm a practical realist; I'm not a foolish optimist. Given the limited level of consciousness of most adventurous souls on Earth and the current state of affairs in the world, it was hard to imagine that this shift would happen anytime soon or that it was actually happening at all!

While pondering this question, a couple of years ago I had some flashes of a new world being created, but they were very unclear. I understood that the reason why these were not clear and detailed was because this is a new world and it has not yet been fully claimed and expressed by humanity. Yes, as we are inherently Creator Beings, we are calling it forth, but it is still in its early stages of infancy. So even if it was presented to me in a clear, detailed way, chances are that I would not be able to fully recognize it, as it is a new world, very unlike the one I am familiar with. It was also pointed out that my reservations about the creation of this new world were founded on the fact that my perspective was still bound by a fixed, linear timeline. As I learned to stand back and reach out to my Higher Self, this perspective would change.

Several months later, I had another flash, but this time it was a bit more detailed and it seemed closer. I saw the outline of a village being built. The sky was bright and much light filled the village. Although it was still quite far away, I could see people working together, joyfully, harmoniously, actually building something. While this was just a flash, perhaps even a projection of my imagination, it seemed very real. I felt relief and hope in the knowing that we are actually making progress, even though it may have been in a parallel timeline or another dimension.

From what I understand, it appears that we have a far greater impact on life, not only here on Earth, but also in other levels of creation. We have much more Creator power than we could possibly imagine as adventurous souls bound by the 3D physical experience. If we have created this world, imagine how much more we can create! What if it were possible? What if it were true that we are participating in the creation of a new world? What will this new world be like? Will it be as wonderful as we would like it to be? We need to claim the more of who and what we are so we can gracefully step through this Gateway and create a new world!

CHAPTER 10 • SOWING THE SEEDS

Whatever you hold as a vision within your heart, whatever you love as that vision, you will bring forth upon this plane. That is empowering. (Jeshua Online—Daily Message)

That daily message, conveniently in line with my writing topic, inspired me to build on what I had seen and then dare to imagine a new world. Maybe it is time for us to put our creative vision to good use—or, to God use—and simply expect that the best is yet to come. Ask yourself: What kind of world do I wish for humanity, for all life on Earth? But first, I needed a little time out to listen to "If I Ruled the World" sung by Tony Bennett. Music will remain always among our greatest gifts! "Okay," as I wiped away the tears, I asked myself: "If I ruled the world, what would it be like?"

In this new world I choose to envision the adventurous souls mending their brokenness and rediscovering their completeness as Divine expressions of Pure Life. No longer in denial of God, fear has been released as the prime directive force. They naturally abide by the principles of harmony, balance, compassion, equality, inclusiveness, peace, sharing and love. Here, there is complete respect for all life forms, including Mother Earth. This is not a world for the adventurous soul who expects competition, challenges and difficulties and is accustomed to being motivated by fear, drama, lack and danger. This is not a world for the one who wants to stand out and outshine others, or the one who wants to be right at the cost of another being wrong. It is a world for the soul who seeks to know the truth of Pure Life as manifested in Creation.

No longer trapped in a state of duality, there are no hierarchies or special groups. No one is better than another; each soul is respected as an equal, unique, creative expression of Source. Since everyone sees the other as an equal, there is a true sense of community, of belonging. It is understood that each one is there for their growth and learning but each one is also there to help the others. No one is ever left out. In the absence of fear, there is no crime, competition, or war. There is no greed or hoarding of money and goods since there is no sense of lack. Goods are shared and distributed among all members of the community. Medical issues are addressed with plants and natural healing techniques. Now learning about their deep innate Divine power, these souls are beginning to experience instantaneous healing for themselves and others simply through visualisation, intent and energy transmission.

In this new world, long-lost innate skills such as teleportation, telepathic communication and energetic manifestation are re-emerging. In this way, far less technology is needed, contributing to a cleaner environment. Food is healthy and produced by the planet. It is consumed more for the pleasure than for the need for survival, since these awakening souls know that Pure Life is the true Source of their existence. Having reconnected with their Higher Self, they are remembering that they are not just physical, incarnated bodies, but that they are beings of energy, vibration, love and light.

What's going on in this new world is that you don't need to wait for somebody to love you in order to be somebody. Reconnected with the Higher Self, no one pines for the one that got away, no one is a motherless child, everyone is embraceable and there is always someone to watch over you. The souls in this world truly know what this thing called love is, they know that love is here to stay, and it is their greatest joy to share it with others and with their home planet. True Love is at the very heart of Being as Divine expressions of Pure Life.

I also came to understand that in this new world, the zodiacal Great Year fades away as there is no longer a need for that inner tug that comes with the backwards cycle of the Eras. It was only there to help with our learning while we ventured out into the world of our own creation, pulling away from our Source, and pretending to exist apart from God. As we step up and reconnect with our Higher Self and become complete once again, a new Era with entirely new attributes will emerge. Fortunately, as inherently creative beings, we are not bound for eternity by our old creations. We remain always free to choose a new way of Being and create something new.

Some will scoff at this utopic new world idea, brushing it off as foolish fantasy. And indeed, it may appear as mere fantasy from the perspective of the world we know. But, is the world as we know it truly what we deserve? Is this what was intended for us by our Divine Creator? As souls who were created in the image and likeness of God, is this the best we can have? Does it reflect our birthright? From our current frame of reference, this bold new world may seem impossible, even silly and unrealistic. But it only seems impossible because our current frame of reference is based on history, memory, programming and experience that is founded on a belief in separation from Source—which is nothing more than a fantasy. For, how can anything be outside of God? How can anything exist outside of Pure Life, the Source of All That Is?

> Be outrageous enough to allow yourself to come alive with the vision of heaven upon earth. (Jeshua Online—Daily Message)

It's about You

This sounds like a bit too much—definitely something H. G. Wells would laugh at. And how long will it take for this impossibly wonderful world to be made manifest? Sounds like it will take forever, if ever! Well, the journey starts Now. In fact, there is only Now since the past and the future are only ideas. Creation—Pure Life in expression—exists in the Now. So it is that our greatest window of opportunity—the Gateway—is available right here, right Now. While looking back on our history can help us avoid repeating past errors, we must forgive and release the past in order to be free to make new choices. While looking to the future can give us hope and inspire us to create something new, something far greater than what we have experienced thus far, it should not be the main focus of our attention, as the future is being created Now. And as Aquarius is all about practical, hands-on experience, being in the Now is entirely fitting.

The truth is that what we are experiencing today is the result of choices, decisions and agreements we have made in the past; what we will experience tomorrow will be the result of choices, decisions and agreements we make Now. So it is that this new world we desire won't just magically appear because it was prophesized in some ancient story. Given that the past must be released and the new must at least be considered as a possibility and eventually accepted and lived, this journey may require a bit of work—okay, a lot of work, a lot more than we might imagine or even want. But, we do want change, right? While new learning is helpful, and in fact is required to loosen the shackles of long-held beliefs and old, familiar ways, it will need to be applied in our everyday lives. We must be ready to work with what resonates with us, and willing to release what no longer works for us. This requires a fair amount of conscious awareness—that is, paying attention to our mindset, feelings, responses and reactions.

How can that be? I certainly didn't create this world. I never agreed to this! And indeed, sometimes it may seem easier to have someone to blame for our circumstances. God created this world; I'm paying for my past karma; we have no power over those in control; those who are in power are controlled by the dark forces. From this perspective there is nothing that can be done and you certainly don't need to hold yourself accountable. It's their fault; you're off the hook. While feeling somewhat vindicated, those who adopt this way of seeing are living as disempowered souls, in complete denial of their essential divinity. They will never find the true satisfaction, the true joy they are seeking.

But how can we change the world when none of our friends, never mind our family members, are into these far-out teachings! How can we fix the brokenness of the world, the unfairness, the control mechanisms, the greed, the corrupt economy, and the never-ending battles and wars? Isn't it unwise, even irresponsible to ignore or deny what's going on in the world? There's no denying this now; it's all around us. Besides, we have no control over what they are doing. It would be foolish to pretend that the darkness doesn't exist. We can't change these things!

And that would be correct. We can't change the world, at least not on the level of the world, and this is not what we are being asked to do. This is probably the toughest pill to swallow, but the fact is that, whether or not we do so consciously, we are always contributing to the whole. The world as we currently know it is a result of the choices, decisions and agreements we have individually and collectively agreed to and made in the past—it is the result of our combined energies. As integral parts of this great adventure, our individual energies merge with the energies of the entire family of adventurous souls. It's like a giant stew, where its flavour depends on the ingredients that are put into it.

If we can simply see it as an adventure into separation from Source/God, or an attempt to live outside of the natural flow and harmony of Pure Life, not as a horrible sin punishable with some form of eternal damnation, it will be easier to correct. All that is needed is a simple shift in consciousness and the willingness to consider that maybe—just maybe—there is something we can do about it. To create a new and different world, we must make new and different conscious choices now, and in so doing, we will make a new and different contribution.

Another important point is that we don't change the world "out there"—at least not directly or wilfully. That's not the way it works. We need to go to the cause, not the result. Here is where more challenges might be encountered, at least for some adventurous souls. This journey is about each individual on Earth at this time. It's not about the world out there, since the world out there is a composite, a blend of what we emanate, or how we are Being. We are not mere physical bodies. As divine expressions of Pure Life, we are complex organisms of spirit, energy, consciousness, mind, intention, vibration, light, love and probably other elements we are unable to conceive of within the physical realm. What we emanate is coloured and filtered through the lens of our desires, beliefs, thoughts, memories, conditioning and emotions, which then colours the world of our creation, hence the importance of paying attention to how we feel and how we interact with the world outside of us.

If we want a new world, we must first Be in a new way, look and see with new eyes, interact with our brothers and sisters from a completely different perspective. In this way, we will contribute new energy; we will Be with Light and Love. This can only happen if we reach out to the more of who and what we are, if we connect with our Higher Self. If being informed inspires you to become more, to Be in a new way so you can make a greater contribution to the healing of humanity in your everyday life, then there is nothing wrong with being informed. Each one here on Earth has a unique role to play, and each one has certain skills, talents and abilities. Now is the time to put these to good use—or God use—a phrase I am starting to like!

To judge, condemn, demean, criticize, denigrate or shame another for their choices, for not agreeing with you or for not being "awake," is to choose to see through the narrow, soiled lens of the small self. From this perspective, the adventure into separation is maintained; what is just an illusion is sustained as a reality. This is essentially the root cause of all problems throughout the universe. While choosing to identify as a small self, we are not likely to see the Divine One, the Child of God in the other. When we limit our vision to what we think we see in the world of form, when we limit what we think we know to history and past learning, we deprive ourselves of an experience of our Higher Self, a much fuller experience of Being. We no longer fully express the Pure Life that is our natural heritage.

When we make choices inspired by the Christ or the Holy One in us, when we stand on a foundation of completeness and Oneness, we are in harmony with the flow of Pure Life. We are then awake to the more of who and what we are and our contribution will be loving, healing, respectful, helpful and uplifting for all. It always comes down to how we choose to see and *Be*. When we step back from the world of separation, when we reach out and plug into our Higher Self, we gain a broader perspective of what is going on in the world around us. This may not be easy to do, at least not at first, given the overwhelming amount of distracting drama and noise from all corners of the universe around us. This step may be challenging for those who derive a certain sense of gratification in being right. There certainly is no shortage of opportunities to point that finger! But this journey is not about being right. It's about giving up the need to be right and showing that maybe, just maybe, there is

CHAPTER 10 • SOWING THE SEEDS

another way of Being. And that other way of Being is compassionate, respectful, peaceful, harmonious, helpful, and above all, loving.

The metaphor of the adventurous souls who have lost their way in a make-believe world of their own creation has been very helpful for me. It makes it much easier to stand back and not get caught up in what "they" are doing, what "they" are saying or how "they" look. It is actually then possible to avoid falling into the trap of judgment. Whether I'm out walking, shopping, on the bus, or crossing paths with someone in the hallway of my condo, I see—or I try to see—an adventurous soul who has chosen to venture out into separation, one who became enthralled by the idea of having a physical experience but who, over time, forgot its essential divinity. Once established in separation, this soul was functioning from fear and all attempts at mending that fear by repeatedly incarnating in physical form through the birthing process simply strengthened the foundation of separation. From this perspective, one can see beyond the distraction of gender, age, attire, race, culture and ethnicity to the truth of who and what they are—children of God in search of Love.

Note that this is easier to put into practice with a stranger than it is with a family member or friend. Familiarity comes with history and memories from prior encounters, but this familiarity is limited to individual exchanges and interactions in the current life. Most of the time, we don't truly know what a person is feeling; only what they are projecting outward. We really do not know what another soul's journey has been like in the past, nor do we know what their learning needs are in the present life. However, knowing that they are at their core a Divine expression of Pure Life that has taken the path of an adventurous soul and simply forgotten their true origins makes it easier to avoid falling into judgment mode. It also relieves us of any preconceived ideas we may have about them, allowing for true vision, but above all, Love.

The challenge now will be to put into practice what we are learning. In time, we come to realize that information or teachings need to be experienced in order to be truly known. It's one thing to read about how to bake bread and believe in a famous chef's instructions.

It's a whole other thing to measure out the flour, add the water, knead it with your hands until the dough is thick and stretchy, let it rest, shape it and then bake it. Now you really know what it's like to bake bread and you feel confident that you will be able to make some for that family dinner next week.

So it is that bit by bit, as we apply new knowledge in our everyday life, barriers are released, our inner brokenness is healed, history is forgiven and past errors and experiences are seen simply as learning opportunities. True knowing then emerges, our perspectives and awareness shift, progress is made and faith in that Inner Self is strengthened. We are on our way to reknowing who and what we are as beloved expressions of Pure Life. The adventurous souls are no longer lost in the forest. We are now contributing to the creation of a wonderful new world. Perhaps we should give ourselves a hug—a nice, big, loving hug—for our courage and determination in the face of this major transformation for humanity. Love is our first major step, and it must be experienced as we move forward into this new world.

So how is this new world created? This new world is created Now, in the moment, as we realign our energies, our vibration, our frequency and our consciousness with the True Self. We do this by first paying attention to our thoughts, reactions, perceptions, feelings and responses in our everyday, ordinary life. With a bit of practice, it becomes easy to identify which part of us is interacting in any situation: the small, separated adventurous soul, or the complete, Divine Self. What is important to know is that the one that interacts is the one that is contributing to the state of the world in the Now moment. Once aware of which part of us is present in the moment, which part we have chosen to align with, it is then possible to make a different choice, as needed.

The voice of the small self is easy to recognize because it does not abide by the principles of unity, inclusiveness, compassion, respect and harmony of Pure Life. No longer experiencing the safety and the all-encompassing Love of Oneness, the adventurous soul living in separation stands on a foundation of fear and must protect itself.

CHAPTER 10 • SOWING THE SEEDS

This establishes a condition of self versus other, or a state of duality, conflict, danger or rivalry. In this imagined state of separation from Source, it must maintain firm boundaries guarding its identity, desires, beliefs and what it thinks it knows. The dualistic nature of life in separation is the true origin of all rivalry, conflict, battles and war throughout the universe. It is simply a projection of the inner battle of the small self attempting to maintain its unnatural denial of God.

The small self needs to be right as this gives it a sense of satisfaction, worthiness, purpose and security. It gives it a ground to stand on, albeit a temporary, imaginary ground. Deep down, it knows that this state of separation is not real and is unsustainable. However, because it is not ready or willing to let it go, it will do whatever it takes to maintain it. This is where its attention is drawn throughout most of its time on Earth. By clinging to separation, it focuses on self-interests, meeting its needs and self-protection. In due time however, it becomes clear that aligning with the small self, while somewhat satisfactory, does not give the soul what it is really looking for: that feeling of belonging and safety found in our true Home and the unconditional Love our heart yearns for.

On the other hand, the Divine Self, the part of us that never fell for the game of separation from Source, has always remained aligned with the principles of Pure Life. It naturally expresses balance, inclusiveness, harmony, respect, understanding, compassion and love. It will never demean, hurt, judge or condemn another. It knows that all are of God, that all are expressions of Pure Life. By connecting with the Higher Self and listening to the Inner Voice, we are inspired by the Creator Energies that naturally flow throughout Creation. Pure Life, Love and Light are then expressed in our words and actions thus sowing the seeds of a new world, a world free of the boundaries, tribulations, fear, lack, limitations, conflict, pain, hurts and traumas of the old.

True power resides in acceptance of the fact that we remain always free to choose which voice we will listen to: the voice of the separated, adventurous soul, or the voice of the Christ Self, the

Higher Self that has never left us. Since there are basically only two options, this makes the healing journey simpler. There is no need for complicated practices and disciplines, or lifelong study. It is a matter of being vigilant for the choices we are making Now. Freedom of choice is empowering; it liberates us from old boundaries, constraints and limitations acquired during our adventure into a world of separation. And always keep in mind that it's not what you do, it's the way that you do it that matters.

If we are like our Creator, created in the image and likeness of God, then we too must have some of its attributes. If we can consider as our starting point that this is the world of our creation, that we are not victims of forces beyond our control, if we can consider that we have contributed and are continuing to contribute to the creation of our reality, then we will become truly empowered. As we accept that we have played a role, and as we become accountable for our past choices, we will have the power to make different choices and create a new world. Not surprisingly, the morning I was working on this section, my inbox was graced with this message.

> This is a time of empowerment, and you are ones who have said at a very deep level, "I will remember my power and I will bring it to bear upon this plane in this time. I will bring it into manifestation as the vision of the One that I am, the beautiful vision." (Jeshua Online—Daily Message)

Sowing the Seeds of a New World

I had not planned on sharing the following stories, because I thought they were insignificant, or too simple. Then I had a couple of experiences that showed me otherwise. Never underestimate the power of the Heart! Nearly forty years ago, I got into the habit of bringing my Walkman whenever I went out for a walk. Depending on how I felt, with a good headset on my head, I'd treat myself to smooth, soothing jazz like Kenny Rankin or Stan Getz, or the classics—Rachmaninoff being at the top of my list. Some twenty years later, I switched from music to lectures and workshops on *A Course in Miracles*. Come rain or come shine, I'd go for my daily walks

CHAPTER 10 • SOWING THE SEEDS

thoroughly enjoying these audios, until one day, I was nudged by my Guides to leave the Walkman on my desk. I found this strange, as I felt kind of safe hiding beneath my headset listening to "spiritual" lectures. Oddly, after having left the house, walking down the street without my headset, I felt naked. When I reached the main street where there was more traffic, I was guided to smile at strangers I encountered. "Smile at strangers? You've got to be kidding, right?" the monk in me replied. It was enough that I was without my headset! But, always open to suggestions, I began to do just that. To my great surprise, it was fun. People smiled back. Sometimes there was a bit of chit chat about the weather, or an item on the shelf in the grocery store.

I never went back to my old practice of listening to music or talks while out walking. Over the years, this practice grew to include comments, or conversations, whenever appropriate. "Oh, I love your hair," or "That's a beautiful dress," or "Your daughter is so cute!" or "You're a great dad, not carrying a phone in your hand and talking to your son!" It was only much later that I realized the impact of these seemingly insignificant exchanges. While walking home from the grocery store with my neighbour, a young man drew our attention. He smiled and said that he loved our attire. We weren't dressed in any fancy way, but he seemed happy to share that with us. "You're one cool dude!" I replied with a thumbs-up for emphasis. I didn't stop to think if "dude" was still a word. But he smiled, we waved goodbye and went on our way. I recalled that incident a few times throughout the day, and each time it put a smile on my face. I realized then that all these people I had praised while out walking must have felt something too.

Then a couple of days later, I had another fun encounter. I had just finished paying for my cucumbers at the self-checkout counter. Instead of cussing at the machine for telling me to "Please remove your items from the bagging area"—I'm just not a fan of machines telling me what to do, no doubt due to the *1984* effect—I turned to the new fellow working the floor that day. I like to get a smile on the way out, so sometimes I make goofy comments like, "Where can I pick up my pay check?" This time I said, "I didn't make any mistakes today! Do I get a raise?" The young man laughed and answered "No, but you can get a hug! My name is Jackson." And he smiled and put his arm around my shoulders! I will always remember that shopping trip!

What the world needs now is more of these small, seemingly unimportant interactions. You feel them, they are real, and they open the heart in us. It feels so much better than judgment, or the need to be right. I see more and more of these exchanges of kindness on social media. They make us feel good. We always get to choose how we will interact with each other. This is one of our greatest freedoms, and the point is that it isn't insignificant or meaningless nor is it without significant impact.

One day, I had a fun chat with the young Walmart employee who was helping my friend process her payment at the newly opened self-service checkout. We had gotten into the topic of technology, and I slipped in a comment about *1984*. I was surprised when he replied that he had read the book. On our way out, he called out and asked if I had read *Brave New World*. "No," I replied. "I'd had enough with *1984*. Instead, I set out to find the answer." He looked at me and tipped his head as though curious as to what I meant. So I asked him, "Do you know where the answer is?" He immediately shook his head. I placed my hand on my heart, tapping gently, and said, "Right here." Then he got it. There was a spark of joy and hope in his eyes. There was an answer to the dark dilemma and it was in the heart—*his* heart, and so a seed was sown.

Imagine being able to look at a brother or a sister with love, no matter their function, their history or their culture. If there is One Source of all life, then each One is of that Source. Find a way to look beyond outward appearances and see the innocent child in them, the one who joined the group of adventurous souls and ventured out into a world of their creation, an experiment of separation from Source. This would extend to all souls, even those in other dimensions or galaxies. Each one encountered is an adventurous soul who has forgotten their Divine origins. Each one comes to Earth through

CHAPTER 10 • SOWING THE SEEDS

the same birthing process and then tries to mend the brokenness, the sadness caused by separation through their worldly interactions, outside themselves. Each one is seeking for the Light, and each one is in need of Love. Be the one who shows the way by turning inward to where the true joy, peace, fulfillment, healing and Love has always been. Be the Light, engage in conversation, and share the Love. You never know what seeds you may have sown in your interactions.

Those brave souls—the pioneers—who are bold enough to open their hearts, release the past and claim their Higher Self have an exciting new purpose in life today. Now standing on a foundation of Oneness and Love of Pure Life, their function is to go out into the world and show how it's done. It's not about preaching a new spirituality or religion; it's about *Being* the Gateway. That's our job today as we step through the Gateway into a new world, as Divine expressions of Pure Life.

God Life, God Love, God Light.
So be it!

What, no Rachmaninoff, no Mozart, no Beethoven? Well I was feeling more of a need for "The Swan" from *The Carnival of the Animals* by Camille Saint-Saëns. What a beautiful piece of music, so uplifting, makes you feel like you can fly away. Okay, I think it's time to go back to my piano lessons. "The Swan" is in there somewhere. Let's enjoy ourselves as we put these new ideas into practice, as we tap into our innate Divine creativity, open our hearts, release the past, open up to the new, awaken to the more of who and what we are and make a meaningful contribution to the creation of a beautiful new world for all life on Earth.

> Live your outrageousness. Allow yourself to smile with the joy that is within, and bring forth heaven upon earth. Empower yourSelf with your remembrance. Empower the vision that you have had, the vision that you would like to see manifest upon this plane. Empower the one Self that we are to come truly alive upon this plane and to manifest in that empowerment, to manifest heaven upon earth. (Jeshua Online—Daily Message)

The Seeds of a New World

Is there more to this life than what I know?
Could I find love here and fulfillment?
A new world waits to be born!
A new me, reborn, made new
Through the love of family and friends,
And inner guidance too!
Delivering me from difficulties
Lifting me up,
Yes, raising me up to all I can be!
What will this new world be like?
It's unknown, that's the wonder of it!
It's always brand new, every moment is.

Let love call out from every mountaintop,
Saying:
"You are loved dearly
You are forgiven
There is nothing you could do
which would make you lose your innocence
There is nothing to fear
We are there for you
Come home
Open your heart to the potential in you
There is so much more to you than you see
So much more to explore
Joy and peace and love and healing
are waiting for you!"

Michael J. Miller

Bibliography

A Course in Miracles. Sparkly Edition.

Bible references are from the New International Version, Grand Rapids: Zondervan Publishing House, 1993.

Coates, Judith. *Jeshua: The Personal Christ,* Volumes I–VIII. Oakbridge University Press.

———. Jeshua Online—Daily Messages.

Edward, Pauline. *Making Peace with God: The Journey of a* Course in Miracles *Student.* Montreal: Desert Lily Publications, 2009.

———. *The Healing of Humanity*, Montreal: Desert Lily Publications, 2017.

———. *Aquarius: The Age of Revelation, Choice and Transformation.* Montreal: Desert Lily Publications, 2021.

Grun, Bernard. *The Timetables of History: A Horizontal Linkage of People and Events.* New York: Touchstone/Simon and Schuster, 1982.

Haramein, Nassim. International Space Federation, Social Media post, July 16 2023.

Herman, Ronna. *Let There Be Light.* Reno: Star Quest Publishing, 2006

Ivanov, Ezra. *Ancient Origins of the Zodiac.* DTTV Publications, 2022.

Jayem. *The Way of the Heart.* Bali, Indonesia: Heartfelt Publishing, 2013. www.wayofmastery.com.

Kribbe, Pamela. *The Jeshua Chanelings.* Booklocker, 2008.

Meece, Alan. *Horoscope for the New Millennium.* St. Paul: Llewellyn, 1997.

Scranton, Daniel. *Ascension: The Shift to the Fifth Dimension, The Arcturian Council.* Volumes 1–4.

Selig, Paul. *The Book of Innocence.* N.Y.: St. Martin's Publishing Group, 2010.

Spalding, Baird T. *Life and Teaching of the Masters of the Far East*, Volume 1. Marina Del Rey: DeVorss & Co., 1964.

Tellinger, Michael. *Slave Species of the Gods.* Rochester: Bear & Company, 2012.

About the Author

Pauline Edward is a writer, retired astrologer-numerologist, speaker, Certified Professional Coach and Group Leader. She is the recipient of a Chamber of Commerce Accolades Award for excellence in business practice. With a background in the sciences and a fascination for all things mystical, Pauline's journey has been enriched by a wide range of experiences from research in international economics, technical writing in R&D, and computer training, to studies in astrology, numerology, meditation, yoga, spirituality, shamanism, ancient history, the Bach Flower Remedies, herbology, healing and reiki. Her profound desire to uncover the truth about the meaning of life has been the inspiration behind her lifetime of writing.

Acknowledgments

I would like to express my heartfelt gratitude for the tremendous help we are receiving during this time of change on Earth. So many guides, teachers and helpers are reaching out and providing us with the knowledge and support we need to make this shift as smooth as possible. A special thank you to those who are serving as channels for our teachers: Judith Coates, Pamela Kribbe, Daniel Scranton, Jayem, Paul Selig and Ronna Herman Vezane, just to name a few.

Not only are we sent teachers when we are ready to learn, we are also sent friends with whom to share the journey. A big thank you to all who have provided support and encouragement for my writing efforts. A special thank you to Michael Miller for helping with the edits and for sharing his wonderful poems. And thank you David O'Donnell for making room for my work during this intense period of change on Earth.

Also, thank you to my friends and clients for asking those questions that push me to find answers to what seem like unanswerable questions, and for sharing the beauty of the unfolding of your Being.

Thank you, thank you, thank you.

Reviews

I loved Pauline's latest book! She writes with such thoughtfulness, it just touches my heart. During the proofreading process, I got the wonderful opportunity to read it several times, and it never got old. Always did I find nuggets of wisdom and love in her inspiring new book. She has grown a lot over the time this book was written, and the reader will no doubt enjoy her journey and her many insights. When we all spread love and grace like she does, the world will become a better place. Thank you for this soul-affirming new book, Pauline! If you read it, you will most likely be blessed by it, as I was.

Michael J. Miller

This book helps remind us of why we are here. A guide to pick up over and over again to help us centre ourselves in these changing times. I highly recommend!

Camille Greenstein, R.TCMP, RAc, PTS, RYT-400

I refer to Pauline's book as the journey towards a healed world. Her story shows us how living our lives with love in our heart is our way to a greater world. If we all lived our journey in this way, what a wonderful world this would be! I highly recommend reading her journey to inspire your own!

Sandra Wiseman

www.ingramcontent.com/pod-product-compliance
Lightning Source LLC
Chambersburg PA
CBHW070055080526
44586CB00013B/1070